MAIL FROM JAIL

GEORGE WESCHE

PAGE PUBLISHING
Conneaut Lake, PA

First originally published by Page Publishing 2023

ISBN 979-8-88654-763-4 (pbk)
ISBN 979-8-88654-771-9 (digital)

Printed in the United States of America

At the time of my arrest, the feds had no facility in Vermont or New Hampshire to house a federal detainee, so they would pay tuition to jails closest to where my trial was to take place. Rutland, Vermont, was where I was to be tried and my lawyer's office was there.

I was bounced around from Rutland, Vermont, and FCI Raybrook, in New York State. Raybrook was the Federal Correctional Institution across Lake Champlain near Bennington, Vermont.

Letter number 1

Johnny,

Well, the *inevitable* happened! I'm going up the river for a while. Not for as long as I originally thought but a few years anyway. Feds dropped some things they had on me. No king pinpoints. No points for being close to the school. Got to go see the shrink for a bit.

Good news. I was taken off suicide watch. I just told her if I survived a week in FCI Raybrook, why would I try to kill myself in this kiddie camp? She agreed.

Raybrook was a real prison, and I will be back there no doubt. It is a level 2 maximum security, and I am minimum. They need to keep me safe while I am there. Contrary to popular opinion, those cells are not to keep inmates in. It's to keep other inmates out. The first night, an inmate who came in with us was beaten and put in the hospital. They came into his cell just after doors were open the next morning and beat him. They put a lock in a sock and beat his ass. Later I heard he owed someone some money.

After sentencing, they may keep my max for a while just to see what kind of a prisoner I will be. Then it's off to a minimum camp for nonviolent offenders. Could be FPC Allenwood, Pennsylvania; Fort Devens, Massachusetts; Danbury, Connecticut. I hear Lewisburg, Pennsylvania, now has a camp. Sentencing June 23, 1994, D-Day!

When I got to Raybrook, an old acquaintance, Beau, was waiting for us. It was good to have him show me around the place. It was intimidating at first.

About 600 inmates, wise guys, Muslims, Arian brotherhood, Crips, Bloods, Dominican, Puerto Rican, Cuban, and Jamaican gangs, and me with the Green Mountain Boys! I also met a bank robber from Boston who knew you! He was on the lamb in Brattleboro and knew Cayene (a band) and Billy. His name is Jerry, but that's not the name he was using up there. He is a drummer, and he hits the street in May. He says he will be up for a visit.

So, I am sitting with my *Vermont posse*, and I go to the salad bar. When I get back, the Green Mountain crew is gone, and I am surrounded by the Cosa Nostra! They run the kitchen. One of them is eating an Italian sandwich that looked great. So Big Mouth Mel says, "Hey, you got any more prosciutto ham back there?" Well, that was it. "Hey Vinny! This kid wants to know if you got any more Italian ham back there." Vinny turns to me and says, "How old are you?" I say, "Forty-seven." Vinny says, "You're too young." My first introduction to the wise guys but certainly not the last.

I had a lot of chances to practice Español mostly with Cubans. Nice people. Illegal aliens and drug dealers. Cisco is writing a letter in Spanish to my Dominican girlfriend letting her know that I am okay, in Spanish.

I didn't argue for bail because I want to get this over with. Every day inside is a time served. Plus, I want to split for the DR soon as possible. I probably won't be able to go for a while.

Bugs and Owl say they are going to come and see me, so jump in the car, boy. Check out the Big House. I never know where I will be, here or Raybrook.

Anyway, I am alright. I can do this. The kids have it the worst. I am getting a free ride. They spend a lot on us Federal prisoners.

"Keep the faith."

Love always
Mel (Big House) Miro

Letter number 2 written from Southwest Regional Correctional Facility
Rutland, Vermont. May 19, 1994

Johnny Boy,

Que passa?

First off let me say happy birthday to Brother Brown, James Brown that is. Still on the good foot! Can I get a witness! Yeah, May 3, 1933.

Ain't this a kick in the head! It's a blessing in disguise because I was going to kill myself. I was getting real bad with the dummy dust. Now I will get help and hopefully not too much time.

This place is a real kiddie camp. Lots of nineteen-year-old kids. Hal, my roommate is up for murder and sexual assault. He raped an old woman on a pool table in Rutland, but he likes me which is a good thing. He had a bad night. I am the oldest in the unit, pod as it is called. "Open the pod bay doors, please, Dave."

The food is not the best. I am losing weight, so I got that going for me, which is good!

I take Spanish, computers, current events today, history, and economics. It's only a few shows. We get to watch CNN over the *edjumacation* unit. It's good 'cause it is quiet. Over in the pod, the kids watch wrestling, MTV (I like), and lame movies which you can't hear. They are all afraid of my roomie for good reason so if it gets too loud, I say something to him, he stands up and threatens everyone's life, and they quiet down for a few minutes!

I don't know if I ever told you about my recurring dream, but in it, you, Bugs and I are all together somewhere (usually in Florida). We are old but still hanging out together at the end of our lives. Interestingly I have had it many times. It is good to know that we still have each other after all these years.

Raybrook is much better than this place. Food was great. The wise guys made the marinara sauce, and you can eat all you want.

Sentencing is June 23. Hope they don't hammer me too hard. "I'm sorry. I learned my lesson and will never screw up again I promise judge." Nothing left to do but pray and bend the judge's brain waves over to the bright side. I was working for the dark side for so long, but now free or incarcerated I will be using the force for good. I have already started talking to these young knuckleheads trying to help them stay out once they get out.

After sentencing, I will be leaving Vermont because there are no federal facilities in the state. Raybrook is an old Olympic village that was converted (Lake Placid). At least I can get some intelligent conversation. I am tired of talking to hillbillies. Plus, your bank robber friend is there!

When Viola (my Dominican wife at the time) heard that I got locked up, she thought I was dead or close to it. She equated it with jail in the DR. She was certain that I would die. They don't feed the inmates. You have to make arrangements to get food.

Her daughter Francia came to visit me and said that I was living better than 80 percent of the people in the DR. Francia put her mind at ease.

I am a nonviolent first offender, so I can't stay at Raybrook. It is a level 2 max. I will go to a camp like FPC Allenwood, Pennsylvania.

I am not suffering here. There are no beatings or physical punishment. If you fight, I don't fight, and you can be sent to the hole. One guy who is here now couldn't stand the kiddie noise. He refused a direct order and was sent to the hole. He said I just wanted to get some sleep. He is here on an assault charge. He caught his wife in bed with another guy. He beat the shit out of him and almost killed her. Just goes to show you what people are capable of given a certain situation.

And then there's Randy! Randy got drunk, took his T-shirt off, wrapped it around his head, walked into a Jiffy Mart, brandishing a samurai sword, and said, "Give me two packs of Marlboro"! The clerk gave him the smokes, and he ran across the street to his apartment! He smoked four cigarettes before the cops showed up. Armed robbery, five years! Jail is home for some folks.

Mom and my sister showed up for a visit today. Dad won't come. He has time. I wrote and apologized to him. We were never very close. He will come around.

We have commissary here every week. You can order shampoo and stuff, etc., get seven free letters a week, but you can only mail in the USA. I write to Viola's daughter in Florida, and she translates and sends them to Viola.

Well, bro, that's enough for this letter. I always enjoy your letters. Me and Jeannie, we read them all.

Love,
Miro

After being bounced around from jail to jail, I finally landed here which is good because my family lives close by. Turns out I will end up spending around a year here before being sentenced and shipped to FPC Allenwood where I served my time.

Johnny,

Thanks for stopping by. Hope you and the Bugman had a nice weekend. I am there in spirit. If I am gonna have to wait six months or more to be sentencing, I want to be close to family before I go on the big ride!

I am getting very horny! Lack of pussy makes you crazy! A piece of ass would be much appreciated. That is the least of my worries.

I like to keep Saturday's visit open for the kids, but they also have visits on Monday. So come on over. There is no visiting list, so all are welcome. I will be home. The kids are getting a special contact visit. I will actually get to hold them. God, I miss those critters.

Well, drop me a line. Send me any news from Bridgeport.

PS, here is some jailhouse graffiti.

"It's all fun and games until someone loses an eye.

Then it's just fun!" That was written on the wall in one of my cells.

Love and kisses,
Mello Bill Miro

Letter number 4 from Cheshire County Corrections
June 19, 1994, Father's Day

Johnny,

Happy Father's Day, you mutha!

Hope you had a good one. The kids came yesterday, and we had a great visit. I am getting ready for my second argument for bail due to Travis being traumatized by this. He was in observation at the hospital in Keene.

This is the worst place that I will see. Federal prison is tit compared to this joint. This place sucks shit through a tube. And I don't mean Vermont bat shit. I mean Mexican...

We have a suicidal fag in our unit. Well, we did. He started a fight in the cafeteria and was placed in the hole. Now he can choke his own chicken in the piece! "Get that clam sauce off my neck." Fagots are everywhere and me without a fly swatter. One fruit in Rutland promised he would only put the *mushroom* in. Help, the snappers are after me! FYI, *snappers* are sex offenders.

Hey, how about OJ Simpson! Not guilty! Ain't that some shit! We have been watching it on TV. It's really exciting to us.

Every night we play volleyball in the gym. It's fun and good exercise. I can do twenty push-ups and also spank my monkey! I asked them if I could go work on the farm, but they told me only a federal marshal can take me out of this place.

Then there's Corey. He stole two pizzas from the delivery lady in Keene. She fell down. He got five years in Concord State Prison. Oh well...

Hey, I've been drug-free for ten weeks. That's the longest for me in years. I went to my first drug rehab meeting here last Friday. They don't have NA here. They send over someone from the Brattleboro Retreat. I like it better than NA. We have a good group. People are serious. Sometimes people attend because it is court-mandated. They go because it looks good to the judge.

I will never do cocaine again.

Hey, when I get out of here, we should take a trip down to St. Pete and catch Lenny D at the Hairy Dolphin. On the way, we can stop and visit Rudy Gumtree. Then we can stop and pick up Laurie the teenage ball freak and Eddie the Long Island drug mooch and watch out for Godzilla in the sewer.

Thanks for writing so quick. Seems like I write letters all the time. That's all I have is time. We should write a screenplay or some jokes. That's how comedy writers write. They sit around and bounce shit off of each other.

Anyway, it's too bad that I can't get my *sluts with nuts* delivered. I can get *chicks with dicks* though. So send it on in!

Love and shit,
Mel

Letter number 5 from Cheshire County Complex, July 4, 1994

Kravetz,

Happy 4th of July, bro. It's just another day to me. Monday nothing, Tuesday nothing, Wednesday and Thursday nothing. Friday for a change, a little more nothing, nothing, nothing, nothing. Not a god-damn thing!

This week I will hear about bail. Say a prayer for me I might get a chance to spend some time with my son, Travis. Plus, I will get out of this shit hole. These people are brain-dead. There is a real police state mentality here. I'll take Devil's Island, the Bastille, any fuckin' place! Hey, do you ever hear from Duck? Say hi to me.

The screws just came through and shook the place down looking for contraband. They turn the whole block upside down, and if they find anything illegal, they write you up. If they find cigarettes or drugs you go to East Block, which is a real cellblock just like in the movies, twenty-three-hour lockdown. That's the punishment block. Of course, they had us federal detainees over there anyway for no reason. Then we spoke to the chief, and a few days later, he moved us to a decent unit. It's still New Hampshire neo-Nazi state.

You have a real good memory yourself. "Such a night." Bugs doesn't have that Boyle on his ass anymore, but being that it is the twenty-fifth anniversary of Woodstock, I am sure that he remembers when Karen accidentally stuck her big toe up his ass!

I haven't heard from my wife, Viola, at all. It takes three weeks one was from the Dominican Republic. I have written her quite a few times but have only received one reply. I am going to call on our anniversary, July 17. Boy, I miss that sugar. I have been having to take things into my own hands.

Well bud, keep on writing. Letters are much appreciated here. Keep the faith.

Love,
Mel

Johnny,

You are the best. You write back the fastest! Thanks, bro. Tonight we get a movie! "Dave." Anything like my brother Dave? Dave's not here. Lynn, my sister, has been writing a lot. She is moving back to Connecticut from Vermont. I am thinking of leaving Vermont (I never did).

I got a great letter from Owl! He is almost out of his bar biz. Cheers. He sent me a joke: Superman is sitting around his house one night watching TV when he thinks to himself, *You know I am feeling kind of horny. I haven't had any in weeks. I think I'll call up Batman, and see if he wants to go on a pussy posse.*

"No can do, Superman. Robin and I are working on the Batmobile." So, he calls up Captain America. "Hey, Cap you up for a little booty?"

"Not tonight. I am home polishing my badges."

"Fuck it. I'm going alone." Off he goes flying around the world on his quest. All of a sudden, he spies Wonder Woman lying on a beach bear naked with her legs spread wide open and her legs sticking straight up in the air. So he thinks to himself, *I could just fly straight down there faster than a speeding bullet, get a little, and be out of there before she knows what hits her.* So down he goes, *bam, bap, boom, boom, zap, zap,* and he is gone in a cloud of smoke! WW jumps up and says, "What the hell was that?"

"I don't know," says the Invisible Man, "but my asshole is killing me!"

Well, you know I was never much on sports. That is until I have all of this time on my hands. I just watched the World Cup with my Dominican friend so *ahora me gusta todos desportes.*

Spoke to Viola on our anniversary. She is okay, sad but okay.

I fell in the cafeteria, and it really hurts. I am on pain pills.

I am going to the hospital in Keene on Monday. I contacted a lawyer, and we may have a lawsuit. I could use $100,000 when I get out of here. You never know. My horoscope says financial gain is close at hand. (Dream on!)

This place is crazy tonight! A few fights and lots of beefs between the more unruly inmates and guards. It seems like violent offenders like me. I shared a cell with Scott in Rutland. He was in for rape, aggravated sexual assault, and murder. I used to say to him, "Gee, Scott these guys are awful noisy. I can't hear the TV." Scott jumps up and says, "Everybody, shut the fuck up, or I will kill you." Suddenly it's quiet! He still writes to me from Rutland. So don't fuck with me. I know people!

Well, that's it for now Johnny. Write back. Keep the faith. Snap your head to the song "I got nuttin' but love for you baby!"

Seg off,
Mel "Big House" Miro

Kravetz,

How's it by you? It's by the balls they get you, at least me! You should have been here last night. Some guy fucked a chicken! Tell me something new. You and Mary are always fighting. You oughta be used to that by now. How did you like the picture of my new bitch?

Enclosed please find some clippings I have collected from the Keene Sentinel. It's not the best source, but it will have to do. What about Michael Jackson and Lisa Marie? Holy shit, Mon. Hey, man shut the fuck up!

Today was my and Viola's first anniversary. She was glad to talk to me. She gets sick when she gets sad. So guess I've been making her sick a lot lately. Her daughter Marisol had her third child a week ago in Lynn, Massachusetts. She is a little girl, and she is an American. The other two are with Viola in the DR. They are beautiful kids. We also have Rowdy Roddy. He is eight years. He was abandoned at the hospital where she works. She just took him home five years ago. Boy, I wish I was there right now.

Hey, write to this address and find out what this government is doing to keep the jails full so that they can get a payday.

> Families Against Mandatory Minimums Foundation
> 1001 Pennsylvania Ave NW
> Suite 200
> Washington DC 20004

It would be cool to get a letter from Mike M., but I haven't yet. He's been where I am going. I also am getting ready to write to Weatherby. My friend Brian and I are facing the same charges and are being sentenced by the same judge, Frank Billings, so we will probably be going to the same place. Brian is cool. He has been to the DR a few times, even Samina.

Well, hope everything is well in Johnny Land! I can't think of much more to say. Bugs writes once in a while, Owl hardly ever. I sent him one of our letters for a birthday card. I thought he might get a yuk. Write when you want, the more the better. Me and Jeanie, we read them all!

Hey, you really think I got no class?

Love,
Mel Bell

Letter number 8

Johnny,

Thanks for the mail. We got our privileges revoked for tonight because people were smoking in here. One real hump of a guard is pissed because he can't catch the culprit. What an asshole. I never smoked a cigarette in my life except for the time you and Duck slipped one in on me disguised as a joint. When I get out here, I'm gonna kick your ass!

By the way, there is some good news. The crime bill that is about to be passed will allow the judges to depart below the mandatory minimums sentencing guidelines in cases of nonviolent first offenders. That's me. Now we delay my sentencing until that new law goes into effect. I am not scheduled to see a judge until November, and it could go into effect in November. Then I could luck out with less than five years. (No such luck. I got sixty-three months). It's better than eleven years which is what they wanted to give me. That was a scare tactic. David S. went to jail yesterday. I don't know when he gets sentenced. After you sign the paper accepting responsibility, you have to surrender yourself into custody. I signed the papers on August 15. The bad news is I won't be making bail. It's all good time though. I get credit for it. The only thing that sucks is that I will be staying here until sentencing. New Hampshire is the worst place to do time.

Frankly I find the whole situation very depressing, Dobie Doo!

To answer your question, after sentencing, I will be going to FPC Allenwood low security.

Love,
Your brother in chains, Mel Miro

Hi, Johnny,

Here's the scoop. I just got my plea agreement from the feds:

Here's the worst, 87 to 103 months. Here's the best, 70 to 87 months. If I get nine years, I will be out in seven. "That's it, partner," she wrote. (I ended up getting sixty-three months). I will probably get my Harley back. Then there's the points I get added on for being close to a school. I think that is figured into the plea agreement. In any case, it's a long-gone Georgie from Bellows Falls! Now he's long gone. Leave them well alone!

I just signed a child support agreement for $50 a month. It seems low to me, but it is probably all that I will be able to afford. If I get into Prison Industries, I should be able to afford that much. (Turns out that Prison Industries is run by the inmates. If you want a job, you have to pay some people off.)

Viola's new granddaughter's name is Noeli, and I hear she is really cute. I got a letter from my son-in-law Tommy. He says Viola is doing fine. The Dominican lawyers who fucked up our marriage felt bad and bought her a TV set. I already got her a VCR. Now she will have something to do on those cold nights without her Signor "Pinga Grande" Mel! God, I am praying for that five-year low end. I can't wait much longer for some lovin'. It is cruel and inhumane. How many times can a guy spank the monkey?

After I sign the plea agreement this Monday, I will be transported back here to await sentencing. After sentencing, I will be transported to a federal facility, probably Raybrook, New York.

After evaluation, I will go to a minimum-security place. They have a bunch in Pennsylvania. I hope for FPC Allenwood. It is a *club fed* with racquetball, golf course, and swimming pool. There are real criminals there. Maybe I can learn something! Just kidding. They have drug rehab and vocational training. (It appears that the feds discontinued schooling of any type the year that I got there.) No more pep rallies (cocaine) for me! I am retiring my schnoz for good.

Have you seen Ice-T's video with George Clinton? Have you seen William S. Burroughs' Reebok commercial? "Strangely scientific!" I like Heavy D. He is my new favorite. I got nothin' but love fuh yah, baby.

I am gonna post this letter.

Dennis and Nancy just left. It was a good day.

See ya!

Mel

Letter number 10

Johnny,

I was watching the Discovery Chanel and they were in the Dominican Republic. Déjà vu. Sosua is the town where I had a gig for you as a drummer in a rock band. After a while tourists want something different than merengue.

The guy was working a lot when the tourists were there. The rest of the time you could take in all of the other Latin sounds and travel to all of the most beautiful places.

Samina, that's where Viola is from. Land of the brown West Indian beauties live. It is going to be a long time before I see that place again.

First, they lock you up for years and still they tell you where you can go once you get out. It's by the balls they get you!

Tomorrow, I get transported to Rutland, Vermont, to cop a plea. I am pleading guilty to the sale of one ounce of cocaine one hundred yards or less from a school. It carries a one-year mandatory minimum, and the feds recommend the low end. That sounds pretty good to you, doesn't it? I would be excepted to this they add the findings of my criminal history report. They are trying to find out how much coke I dealt in my career. I say 3.5 kilos. The informant says I have been at it since the beginning of time! Anyway, the cops who are putting away are recommending leniency so that carries a lot of weight with the judge

I could get five years. I could get out in three. I have been in for four months, and it will be seven months by sentencing.

Love,
Mel

Kravetta,

What's up, dude? I haven't written for a while because I had a lot to do this week. I was transported to Rutland. On the way to court, we had to stop where Sagers is to pick up a dude. He said that all Sagers does is burp, fart, snore, and talk while they are trying to watch TV. They send him to his room!

Anyway, now I should be sentenced to one or two months. They came last week and did my presentencing investigation. That's where they ask if you understand the trouble you caused and the damage you did. Well, I do, and I am sorry. I think it went well. PSI, people are the probation department, and they carry the most weight with the judge. I just want to get this over with. Let's get this started and get to a real prison.

I just wrote Duck for his birthday. I didn't have a card, so I sent him one of your letters. That's better than any card.

Hey what does being in the Mafia and eating pussy have in common? One slip of the tongue, and you are in the shit! The summer is over. I watched them plant the garden, and now I am watching them harvest. At least we get fresh veggies.

August 24th

Good morning. I got burnt out on writing last night. I had to give the old synapse a rest. I am all cranked up with coffee now, my new drug of choice. "Let's buzz a while." I am sitting in front of the tube looking at the weather forecast that I won't be able to enjoy. At least I have MTV. Good-looking babes from across the land. Only thing is I could be their father. It's kind of like a bandstand-soul train merge. Rock on with your bad self.

All the young guys think it is a cool saying. They were interested to hear that James Brown said it twenty-five years ago. We got one kid in here. He's a smart kid. He is nineteen. He's like we used to be.

He identifies with the brothers. He likes to rap all the time. All the time bustin' rhymes. So, I walk up to him and say, "It's like a jungle out there. Sometimes I wonder how I keep from going under rock star doll baby mamma."

"I can be very casual!" So I am the coolest father figure in the joint! I got a letter from Lynn. She says my parents are really bummed. They don't want the family to know about me. They said that I was in the Dominican Republic. I don't know where I will end up, too soon to tell. Lynn is planning a visit real soon. She said she will call you.

Well, I am getting an hour outside, so I am going to take advantage of it.

Keep the faith.

Grand Master Mel, the new minister of the super heavy funk! Downtown brown town.

Shonnie,

'Sup bro! Same old, same old, on this end. Just waiting for them to come and get me for sentencing. Right now, would be good. Let's get this show on the road! I'm tired of this small-town jailhouse. I want a world-class prison.

We actually have a section exactly like movies. It's where they put you for punishment. I was there for nothing. I'm public enemy number 1 you know. One of the marshals who transport me said that I had the same cuffs on that they used for Noriega. They took him to McDonald's, and he had a chicken sandwich. Now where else can you hear news like this?

Travis was here on Saturday. He is not really good with info but he said you had an article about Sagers and me. What's the story? Send an article or paraphrase, please.

I have a new favorite video. *Pop, pop, pop*, go the pistol, *Bang, bang, bang*, go the gun. Prince, and it's hot, hot, hot. Check it out. I like his new style. He's cool, he's bad, we bad, I ain't so bad, but I'm clean. I'm tired, but I'm clean!

Remember we had a guy here who cut off his pecker?

Well, he is back and lives two doors down from me. Across the hall is a delayed stress manic and a psycho killer.

Quest que cet? We complain because they kept putting young guns in here. So instead, we get manics. But I'm okay!

Today is Oprah's birthday. Aretha, Patti LaBelle, and Gladys Night all sang on her show. Great show! God, I am starved for a live show. James Brown and Jerry Lee Lewis.

Better not die before I get a chance to see them again.

Here are some items of interest from the home skillet.

Owl is a man of leisure, and he and Bugs are planning a trip upriver.

Keep the faith.

Mel

Maceo,

Blow your horn. Don't play me no trash. Play me some popcorn! Remember Brother Brown knows what's best to get out on the floor, and let the Boogie do the rest!

Yup summer is gone just like that. We ate corn on the cob, and yesterday the boys brought in a bushel of apples from the orchard. Time for football. It's going to be another building year for my giants. Guess I will have to route for the Patriots or the Skins.

Viola won her court case in the DR to get ownership of her house. So now we have two houses. (I ended up quitting claiming my house in Vermont to my ex and my kids). Until my ex pays me the $24,000. She doesn't have any money, and it will help the kids.

That dude that got popped in Richmond, New Hampshire, with two tons of Colombian weed is here now. He has some outstanding beefs with the feds. He was also in federal prison before. So he is in deep poo-poo. Not a bad dude—old hippie like us.

Then there's Jerry (little Jerry is five feet two inches). Jerry likes to swim around in the shallow water and rub up against the little girls. Jerry says, "At least they weren't little boys." You sick bastard! The cops saved his life. It seems that the girl's fathers were administering a little on-the-spot justice when the cops arrived. I am having a lot of trouble finding any compassion in my heart for O'l Jerry. He is over on the jail side where he has a new job. He is a punching bag!

Thanks for the holy cards man. Faith in God really helps. There is a girl in here named Lisa, and she has a lot of problems. Her father gave her her first shot of heroin when she was seven then he raped her. That's just the beginning. Anyway, we are friends, and she put me on a prayer line. They pray for me every time

I go to Rutland. It seems easier that I am a believer in Jesus Christ and as Jerry Lee (who is hell when he's well) says, Jesus is on the prayer line. Call him up some time! The line is never busy. Call him up sometime. I got a lot of hope. This little chapter in my life has saved it.

Have you ever of Bubba? He is kind of the *Dear Abby* of prison.

Dear Bubba, the guy in the cell next to me says I have a nice ass. He always sits next to me in the chow hall. Are we moving too fast? I have my reputation to think of. I don't want to get written up for receiving swollen property or assault with a friendly weapon!

Hey you, drop the skittles, and move away from the jungle gym!

We got a guy in here from New York City named Brian. He's my best buddy in here. You may have seen him on *Unsolved Mysteries*. He was a pot grower in Vermont who disappeared when the feds found his crop. He went to California and got a job working with horses. He ended up working for William Randolph Hearst Jr.'s ex-wife.

Also, Patty Hearst's stepmom. She is coming to visit (celebrities).

Brian used to have a sailboat and traveled all over the world.

According to him, 80 percent of the shit they said about him on *Unsolved Mysteries* were lies. He has a multimillion-dollar lawsuit against UM.

Well, brother Yonz gets your tickets while they last. I am out of here anytime now—off to club fed. Love to see you before I go. Down the road, I got to go! We gonna take it on out real soon.

Soon I take the *Fantastic Voyage*. If you can't stand the heat, get out of the kitchen; we are on a mission.

Love,
Mel

"If I wanna be freak n' steal it on the weekend ain't nobody's biznez."

The screws let us stay up an extra hour to watch football. We had to write a formal letter. Get me to a real prison. *Mas pronto possible*!

Another guy in here was out in Minnesota. He suffers from seizures. They have a prison hospital near the Mayo Clinic. He was in with Jim Bakker. Praise the Lord. Jim was on TV last week wearing cowboy boots and a Harley shirt. Is nothing sacred Jim?

Listen, buddy. Don't send me any photos or stuff like that. I am getting ready to leave here. When I get to an FCI (Federal Correctional Institution), I go in with nothing. They take the clothes off my back and mail them home. I won't even have a stamp till I get a job, or somebody sends me some money. If you send me pictures now, they will just send them back. So keep them until I get a more permanent address. Life is a test. It is only a test. Had it been an actual life you would have received further instructions as to what to do and where to go and what station to tune to. Remember, Kravetz. That was your favorite saying.

Also, I am sending back those holy cards for you to keep. I want them back. They were nice. God is God—you can name him your mammy if you wanna!

Well, I am going to mail this to you today. I was waiting to see if I got a letter from you, but none came. I got a letter from my sister. She said she spoke to you.

Be cool. Write soon.

Mel

Dr. Jerry, my champion,

I just received a letter from Brother Luke, the lowest of the Flames. I am sending your letter to him so he can show Owl. My friend Owl was very sick at the time.

I got into trouble here for passing a note to a female inmate with Owl's name so she could put him on the prayer line. Unbelievable, they can kiss my ass. My brother is down, and I am going to help in any way I can.

And don't forget the balls; they ain't orphans you know.

I am up early today as usual, but today is the 15th and every 15th, I call Viola to say hi. It's always kind of hard because I miss her, and she is really sad.

Francia, Viola's daughter may be modeling for Avon in one of their catalogs. Nancy Bazin is one of their reps, and when they were looking for Latina models, she thought of Franny. Maybe she will get a chance to shake her little brown tush on the catwalk!

Bugs and Grace will be here on Saturday. Maybe I see you too. I want some good news about Owl. I am praying every day for him. Hootzilla, the blindest of the Flames!

May he make a comeback on national TV.

Just come back. I just want to reach out and bite ya—not just a part but all of your heart. And when I sing that little part that stings you in your heart, I want you to scream! Have a momma for me. No matter what you doin', it got to be boss. Some of those lyrics can be fun but often dangerous! I get my letters mixed up. Send them to each other. Gad the colors! Boy, the Lettuce Brothers (it is what we call each other) never meant more to me than they do these days. Remember when we opened for Lloyd Floyd and the Untouchables at Spoons Record Store?

Well, I gotta go down to the Bridgeport Arena to set up a match between you, Luke vs Gorilla Monsoon and Sweet Daddy Siki. I want you to *destroy*.

Love and kisses,
Bobby Davis

Yo, bro,

Que passa, mi amigo? Espero que tu es Bueno. I am still here. Great visit last week. Don't know what I would do without the Lettuce Men and my kids. I probably would just say fuck it.

Haiku:

> The steel door crashed again and again,
> The young man cried out in furry.
> Visiting room filled with my children
> Glass barriers
> Sadden our hearts

I wrote this. Don't tell me I got nothing to do. Every day I say a prayer for Owl. Have you got any news?

Well, we got a celebrity inmate. Gordon McRae the diddler (child abuser) priest is here for aggravated sexual assault. He is on appeal so there is no bail. Good! Two more days on suicide watch, and he goes into the population with the unsentenced! That's where I was, with a capacity of twenty-eight persons. They have twenty-four over there now. Living on top of each other, lots of fights. They have their own brand of rehab for diddlers (snappers). It's called punch therapy! They might even put him in protective custody or in here with us—the tuitioned boys—maybe he can go next store to Less Johnson, the dickless boy! The revolving door of mystery guests keeps on keeping on!

Hey, where does "When you are born cheap you die cheap" come from? ("Women behind bars": a play by John Waters).

I talked with my mother yesterday. My niece Sara was attacked in her apartment in Providence, Rhode Island. The guy cut her, but she wasn't raped thank God. She needed an operation because the knife severed some tendons. She will be alright in time.

My daughter Gracie went up to see Sagers last weekend. They have contact visits. The guy who runs this shit hole is devoid of any human compassion. I think he squats to piss.

Here is a message for Angelo. Tell him nobody ever called Pablo Picasso an asshole. Not in New York.

That last letter was a blinding scorch! I am sending it to the Bugman Institute Archives.

I just came from seeing my drug counselor. I always feel better after seeing him. My PSI is complete so it should not be much longer till I leave. I know I keep saying that. Get me out of here.

The other day, Geraldo Rivera had John Bobbitt on his show. (Remember his wife cut his dick off while he was sleeping?) I bet you I was the only person in the country who was watching that program with a guy who actually did cut off his own pecker, Cliff Roby. The shrink came yesterday and declared him clinically insane. The Keene Sentinel wants an interview. They have been after him for eight months. He told them to fuck off. Can you imagine? Talk about *putting your shit on the street.*

We also had Gordon McRae (the diddler priest) in here again for a week. They took him out and put him in isolation. They had to watch him all of the time.

The kids are coming to visit today. It is a contact visit. That will be great. Coupled with the completion of my PSI, I feel like it is the end of this chapter. It is time to move on, and I am ready.

Who was the first computer operator?

Eve, she had an Apple in one hand and a Wang in the other!

I just had my computer class, came upstairs, and was busted for having two towels. They are gonna give me life. Yesterday they had an open house here for the local school kids. (About 600 kids across the street doing little workshops). I look out the window, and who do I see? Jim Mort. How come he is still out? That cheese-eater! (One of the biggest dealers in Southern Vermont).

I gotta get ready for my visit with the kids.

Mel

Brother Yonz,

Thanks for the news about Owl. Everyone has been so good about keeping me up to date. Really wish I could see him.

You are right. A Lettuce Brother reunion is definitely in order for the not too distant future. And Owl will be there. I have no doubt that he will pull through. I think I will write him a letter after I finish this one. Lynn wrote about the pool tournament at the *bugatorium*. A long time coming.

My situation remains unchanged. I still need some pussy. Miro was its greatest lover. He even adored the odor!

I still got the feathers in my teeth!

Lynn sent me some great pictures of the kids she took in black and white. They are actually laughing. I got a contact visit with them last Friday. It was great. If I was in Vermont, I could have contact visits every visit, but not in Nazi Land, New Hampshire. We must have order at all times. They are the brain police!

Say hello to J. R. next time you see him. I am not going to be able to write Mike W. and vice versa while we are both incarcerated. Maybe I will have Lynn forward a letter to him. I haven't been writing much. I am kind of in a slump. Here I sit broken-hearted. You know the rest.

It is 6:00 a.m., and I am in the dayroom watching *Flipper*. Mindless entertainment. We saw *True Romance* Wednesday night and *Philadelphia* last Wednesday.

Well, bro, keep those cards and letters coming. And big-legged women keep those dresses down. You got something up in there make a bulldog choke a hound!

May the longtime sun shine on you, all love surround you, and the pure light within you guide your way home.

Love,
Mondo Mel

Kraveta,

The lawyer called me yesterday. I signed and accepted the agreement. I am getting six and a half years or less. They recommended the low end of sixty-three to seventy-eight months. Subtract 108 days a year of good time and six and a half months' time served. I spend at least a year in a halfway house. Also I may be eligible for a two-point safety valve reduction which would bring it down to four years instead of four.

Also, the judge doesn't have to go by the guidelines at all. He can suspend the sentence. My lawyers plan to argue for a reduction in court. My presentencing agreement could not have been better considering. So keep those prayers coming, and you might be seeing my smiling face before you know it. If the time is not too much, this intervention in my life will be just what I needed. I feel great. I am getting treatment. Everything is positive.

Good news about Owl. I got a letter from you and Bugs on the same day. Bugs says Owl is a tough *Guinea bastard*, and I agree. You could hit him in the head with a shovel; he wouldn't know! Thank God he is back. The Lettuce Brothers can survive to make another comeback.

The lawyer says within the next two weeks I am long gone from Kentucky. I already know I am lucky! But keep writing because I won't believe it till I see it.

I love you, brother, with your bad self. Love, peace, chicken grease. The Lettuce Brothers got my back!

Love,
Miro

Johnny,

Keep these pictures and addresses for me, will ya? They are going to take them away from me when I get to federal prison. You can mail them back once I know for sure where I am going.

Hey, did you see they are auctioning off Mafia boss Tony "Big Tuna" Acardi's house in Chicago? Great name, "Big Tuna"!

Every day I wake up and hope that they are coming to take me to court, do me and get it over with.

Nebadon (my oldest son) came to see me last week. That was the last time I was to see him alive. He died of a brain aneurism on March 3, 1995. I miss you, Neb.

TV dinners by the pool, got another year of school. It's a bummer every summer—cabbage is a vegetable. I think I am rutabaga—all of those vegetables worshiping together in the church of their choice. Only in America!

Uncle Meat, Mitch, and Leona. I'm gonna *booglarize* you, baby (*Trout Mask Replica*). Clean up the air, and treat the animals fair. I'm gonna grow fins and make love to a mermaid. Maybe it's your hairspray or something. Who could imagine that they would freak out in Kansas? Little Umbrellas, Drumbo, Zoot Horn Rollo—plastic people. Oh, baby, now what's got into you? My mind is all over the place today, just riffing!

Woman trouble, hey. Next time she acts up, do what Mr. Natural does. Just shove your dick down her throat. What does it all mean, Mr. Natural? Don't mean shit! Once you get passed the smell, you got it licked. Hey, let's watch some TV. Why bother? I am Despair Comics, too fucked up to love. Right on, free on, out of sight! Fat Freddie's cat. Bite me crank, matey. The heads the best. Stop, stop. Turn it off. My mind is melting. Visions of Terry and the bull dykes cruising into Westmoreland, busting me out of the slammer, and taking me to Daytona for a fuck fest. Harley Man is there!

Turn that thing down, voodoo child. Make love to you in your sleep—Spanish castle magic. Hey, Joe. God's grace of infinity—Venus which is red—have mercy. Tire tracks all across your back, I can see you had your fun. Cross town traffic, so hard to get through to you. Threw the bums a dime in your prime. Look out, kid, it's something you did. God knows when but you're doing it again. Twenty years of schooling, and they put you on the dayshift. I wrote that in my Cadillac—good car to drive after a war. Whew, somebody stop me! Get well, Owl. I knew that you could. Zip-coded. Clark Terry, Thelonious Monk, Philly Joe Jones. Still my favorites.

I love you, Bro.

Thanks for being...

Mel Bell

Letter number 20, Cheshire County Corrections, October 25, 1994

Kraveta,

Well, it is official. At 10 a.m. on November 10, in Rutland, Vermont, I get sentenced.

Well, I didn't send this letter sooner because I didn't have any news. So that's some news.

Here is some more news. I was out in the exercise yard with some guy who lives in Jaffrey, New Hampshire. I told him that the first hippie that I ever knew lives in Jaffrey, New Hampshire. His name was Jeff Vulte. He said, "Who?" I repeated the name. He was from Westport, Connecticut, years ago, and we used to hang out.

The guy says, "I know him. He lives on the top of a mountain in West Swanzey, New Hampshire." All he ever does is smoke pot and drink beer! Good guy, that Jeff. Remember when we used to go to his apartment to get high and watch you and Sue Dudko beat the shit out of each other?

Also here is some more hopeful news. My lawyers sent me a draft of my draft for a downward departure from twenty-six points where I am now to seventeen. If the judge goes for it, I will only have to do twenty-four months (he didn't go for it). Now that's more like it. I would just have enough time to do drug rehab and halfway house. That is as good as it gets. Major coolness, dude! Keep praying and don't stop till November 10.

All you ever do is blabber and smoke!

Well, bro, the good news is I could be back at large sooner than I thought.

Brother Mel

J. K.,

As you may have already guessed, I am still here. The whole world knows I'm here. I'm your hoochie coochie.

Man, everybody knows I'm here! I'm drinkin' TNT. I'm smoking dynamite. I hope some screwball starts a fight, 'cause I'm ready—ready to leave. Something came up with the marshals last week, so they couldn't move me. I get to spend another weekend in this hole. It's freezing. The screws locked us all up in the gym with no coats and no heat for three hours while they searched the whole place. They took my extra blanket so I get to freeze tonight.

The marshals said they would come for me definitely this coming week. I will probably go to FCI Raybrook for starters. Any fucking place will do.

Tonight is Friday, and they stuff this place with weekenders which means there will be twice as many guys in here everywhere, clothing change, chow—it all sucks. Help me, somebody. Ain't no life nowhere!

"Cheap motherfuckers here," says Cliff Roby (Les Johnson). You remember he cut off his pecker? He just walked into my cell to fart on me. He's crazy, but I like him better than most others. He's more sane than a lot of them. I was having a conversation with him about weekenders. I said, "I hate them because you can't jerk off in peace with them around." Cliff says, "I can't jerk off anyhow!" I have no response. "I have to stick a bottle up to where my dick used to be to piss." I asked him if he had wet dreams. "Once or twice a month. Big fucking deal," he says. "No pussy for the rest of my life" God, he has told me all about what was going on in his head when he did it. It's weird. He just snapped. He is okay now, but it is hard to find a reason to live. I don't think I would want to. I love all the women! Eat more chicken than any man alive. I even adore the odor.

Well, I keep saying this, but I hope the next letter you get from me is from my new destination.

Love,
Melvin

Kravetz,

The day before Thanksgiving, I was transported to Manchester, New Hampshire, by the marshals. They took us to an airstrip and surrounded us with military personnel armed with AK57s.

Out of the sky dropped the prisoner jet *Conair* carrying approximately 150 male and female prisoners. They loaded me, Sagers, and four others on the plane, and off we went to Otisville, New York, where I got off. The last stop was El Reno, Oklahoma, where I think Dave got off. I am at Otisville now but not for long. I was told FPC Allenwood. FPC stands for Federal Prison Camp. My counselor saw this fat middle-aged man surrounded by blacks, Rastas, Crips, Bloods, you name it, and took pity on me. He put me in a better unit with an older Chinese man. I later found out he was one of those illegal aliens who was caught when Sister Ping, the famous Snake Head (people smuggler), was forced to run a freighter, the Golden Venture, up the East River and beach it in Rockaway, Long Island. All the refugees jumped off and tried to run into the neighborhoods. The cops caught most of them, and here they sit. I think he is a nice guy, but I can't talk to him.

So Cesar takes me under his wing and moves me in with him. He speaks English. Also I have met Lebanese and Pakistanis who seem okay. The Chinese are becoming a show of force. They get really pushy when they are together.

I am considered a short-timer here with only a five-year sentence. I came in with a dude doing three consecutive life sentences plus thirty years. He got caught on the New Jersey turnpike with a tractor-trailer filled with cocaine, also two pallets of cash. The judges are out of control. Where is the justice?

Send me back my shit would you? Even if they move me from here, they will forward my stuff now that I am in the system. I need my contact list and my pictures.

My mother is sending the article about Owl that was in the Bridgeport Post, kind of like the one on Monk's family. I hear Owl is home but in a wheelchair. That poor guy can't catch a break.

I am no longer Mel Miro or any variation on that theme. I am 03558-082. So when you mail me anything, this number must be included.

Well, dude, that's what is new in the continuing saga, *The Life of Mel*.

Your brother in chains,
Mel

Letter number 23 FPC, Allenwood, Montgomery Pa. December 12, 1994

After enduring *diesel therapy*, being bounced around from facility to facility by bus, I am finally at Allenwood Prison Camp, Montgomery, Pennsylvania. On the way, I spent a day or two at FCI Schuylkill and "the Big House" Lewisburg Penitentiary.

I was kept out of the population there thankfully. That's where all the real bad dudes live. There are lots of ways to die there without doing a thing. All the mobsters are there any a various assortment of deviants.

Johnny,

Well, I'm finally here. FPC Allenwood, Pennsylvania. Better food, lots of freedom, no walls or fences or razor wire. I am in with a better class of criminals. I've never seen so many *Wall Street* journals in one place in my life. This beats hanging out with gang bangers. Charlie Kelton is here from Westminster, Vermont. Tuba is down the road, and Beau is about a mile away. He was here but got into a fight so they put him back behind the fences.

Allenwood is a prison complex. There is a penitentiary, a medium (FCI), and a low or prison camp. Aldrich Ames is in the penitentiary. He is our celebrity inmate. He was a spy. He got a lot of American spies killed in Russia.

I was only at Otisville for about five days. This is my designated place. They have a residential drug treatment facility here. I will stay here till I go through that. Then on to a halfway house.

They really have too many people here. It's a pain in the ass but much better than New Hampshire. I am on a top bunk with a locker. I used to have my own cell. Cheer up, it's only for two years. I will be here until I get to do the 500-hour drug program. It would cost $54,000 at Betty Ford. Then I could be shipped to a camp closer to Vermont (never happened).

I got my job assignment today. I am in food service. I got on a list for Prison Industries where you can make a little money. (That also never happened).

Write soon, Johnny. Your letters cheer me up!

Mel

The joke here is, hey do you have any fences there? Yes, there's one around the tennis court!

Letter number 24, FPC Allenwood, Montgomery,
Pennsylvania, January 6, 1995

'Supp, keed!

That is my impression of a Dominican gangster!

Happy New Year! I'm chillin' like a villain with my gangster homies! Ain't no shame in my game! "Hey, Leroy, your mama, she calling you man." It's New Year's Eve. Another year has passed. Happy Birthday, bro. How old are you now? Can you still get it up? I don't bother with it anymore. No loving for me for a long time unless I can get myself transferred to Danbury. There are 700 female inmates there. Dream on. Guess I will stick with Thelma thumb and her four sisters for now.

You should be getting your visitor questionnaire soon. Fill it out and get your asses down here. You got to check this place out.

I talked to Dennis and Nancy last night. It was Dennis's birthday. He turned forty. He went and got my Harley back from the DEA assholes. She is back where they took her from waiting for my return.

I am getting bored with the Green Mountains myself. All you have up there are rich old hippies and hillbillies. One of the half-way houses is in New York City. I was thinking about taking it. It is a free place to live for five months. Most of the guys here are from the New York area. It is refreshing to be around diverse people again—blacks, Latinos, Mafia, insider traders, and tax frauds. One guy, from Statin Island, said he would help me to get a job if I wanted to move to the city. Who knows what will happen? But like I said, twenty years is a long time to live in one place. This is definitely a crossroads in my life. Time for a new chapter. "It's life and life only," Bob Dylan said. There are a lot of variables: Maybe the Lettuce Brothers could start a corporation or something: "Mondo Intenso Enterprises."

Well, bro, I got to go to work. Today I made 350 pounds of mashed potatoes and yesterday 180 pounds of rice pilaf. Chicken necks and chicken feet, chicken necks are all I eat!

Gotta go.

Keep the faith, you dirty heuer.

Love,
Grand Master Mel

Johnny,

I got a medical three-day idol because I got the flu. It really sucks being sick here. The heat in the dorm is fucked up. I had the chills all night. I am also trying to get out of the kitchen. I got hurt in the New Hampshire jail. My neck is all screwed up, and I get shooting pains in my arms and shoulders. The kitchen work is too manual and also too long. I need one of those cushy jobs. I am working too hard for those twelve cents an hour. I have a chance to work in the power plant at the prison complex. (penitentiary). That's where Beau is also Aldrich Ames, our celebrity spy. There is access to a typewriter and some food. I am going to make a sick call again tomorrow and see if I can get out of the kitchen. I would be able to stay up all night and write. I don't even have my own desk yet. My cubie is a real unfriendly jerk. He goes home on Monday, and I will get his desk and closet space.

Viola's daughter is in the DR now collecting her two oldest kids, Pedro and Stephanie, and bringing them to Lynn, Massachusetts. Great kids. Real cuties.

Hey, don't forget to send in your visitation forms. Bugs has his in place. You need to be approved or you can't come to visit.

Well, brother, not much news to report. I ain't seen my main squeeze in over a year. You know I got the blues!

Nine below zero, and I ain't got a lousy dime.

Keep on the good foot!

Love,
Mel

On March 3, 1995, I was on the compound when my name was called over the loudspeaker. I was to report to the chaplain's office. That is never good news. It usually means someone in your family has passed away. As I walked over I was thinking in my mind that my dad had passed. When he told me that my eighteen-year-old son Nebadon was dead, the bottom dropped out. I couldn't believe it.

How could this be? I got on the phone with my ex-wife, and she told me Neb died of a brain aneurism. He was only eighteen years old. He died in his sleep on his mother's bed. The last time I saw him was at the New Hampshire jail.

The saying is true. You should never have to bury your children. It should be the other way around. Now came the most complicated part, dealing with the BOP (Bureau of Prisons) to see if they would let me go to the calling hours in Bellows Falls, Vermont. It was easier for me than most. I was a nonviolent first offender so I didn't need a prison guard chaperone. My dad sent airline tickets, and I was to fly to Bradley International in Hartford, Connecticut. I am from Connecticut, and some friends were going to pass right by on their way to Vermont. They picked me up, and we made it to Neb's wake. It was so sad seeing all of Neb's friends and all of Susan and my friends. My other two kids, Grace and Travis, were all in tears. It was great to hug them and kiss my kids.

I was only given a thirty-six-hour furlough and had to be back to Allenwood, or I would be considered an escapee. I was cutting it close because I couldn't leave. As it was, I couldn't go to the burial. My friends Dennis and Nancy threw me in their car, and we sped back to Bradley. That was a hell of a ride but we made the flight. At least I got to say goodbye to Neb. A guard met me at the Montgomery airport and drove me back to prison. I made it on time.

Johnny Boy,

Well, I am back at the ranch or should I say back on the reservation. I made it back on time. I had a driver waiting for me at the airport. It was great to see you, bud! I had such a warm feeling that day at the funeral parlor. There was a lot of love in that room. Boy, that Neb was quite a dude, a real son of flower children. He was only around for a short time, but he made quite a hit with his friends. I am so proud of him. I will miss him always, but I am very thankful to have had him as long as I did. God has other plans for the boy, but as Neb used to like to say, "I'm on a mission from God!" (Blues Brothers). I guess he went to get the band back together! Wherever he is, he's on a mission, a fantastic voyage. And you know whatever it is, it's got to be funky!

Bugs sent me a beautiful letter a couple of days ago. It was one for the archives. It was a beautiful eulogy to the "Bone Head." It made me cry. Neb was a chip off the old block, and he loved doing the same things that we did at his age. He was a constant source of pride and joy for me. He was kind and compassionate, rare qualities in a teenager. *He will be missed!*

I got some good news about the drug program. I guess we will be getting a year off for doing it. That puts me on the street in May of 1997 instead of 1998. That's about eighteen months off. I will take it.

In your next letter, would you please tell me all that went on after I left the funeral parlor? Did you go over to the house! I am still trying to get one of those posters that Bill made for the kids.

That's it for now. I love you, but you knew that. Be cool.

Mel

Johnny,

Sorry, I don't write as much anymore. Now that I am down here, I have a job and stuff. In the other jails, I did nothing every day except write letters. But I am still funky! Owl sent me *Rolling Stone* and *Money* magazine. Thanks for the Easter pictures. For me, Easter was just another day. I didn't have to work which was good. The movie was *Shawshank Redemption* which was a hit in here. "Come and get me you dirty screw!"

I haven't heard from Bugs or Owl lately. I spoke to Lynn on Easter. She didn't recognize my voice. She thought it was you. Stay away from my sister, or I will kick your ass! Ha ha.

I talk to Gracie and Travis a lot. They seem okay. I really miss those critters. I hope they make it down soon for a visit. I haven't had a visit with them since last summer. It sucks but I am in pretty good spirits.

I got a couple of letters from Weatherby. A guy who spent a couple of years with him in FCI Butner, North Carolina (Lucky), and I are trying to get him to transfer here. We might as well be locked up together. He has camp status now. He should have had it all along, but he got in a little *beef* at Otisville. It would be good to have him here.

There is a guy in here from Boston who is one of the best guitar players that I have ever heard baring none. He says that he has enough material for an album when he gets out. He says he plays Latin jazz. I have never heard him play any of that, but I have heard him play just about everything else. He has been to the *common ground* in Brattleboro. He got really excited when I told him that my best friend was a jazz percussionist (also peckerhead!) He has worked with J. Geils etc. Don't be surprised if he looks you up.

Better days are coming. We shall overcome.

Write when you get the time.

Miro

Letter number 28, FPC Allenwood, Montgomery,
Pennsylvania, May 5, 1995

Johnny Boy,

Que passa? Thanks for the picture of Lana Turner. It is a classic. I am going to give it to one of the old cons. His name is Al. He has been in jail forever. He and his buddy Salvatore talk about the good old days at the Copacabana.

I just got a great letter from Lynn. She sent me an old picture of Nebadon when he was about one-year-old sitting on a bulldozer up at her and Billy's place in New Hampshire. It is priceless.

Not too much to report. All I do is go to work in food service where I am in charge of the soup bar. I keep it shining clean for the 900 inmates that use it. I do my daily four-mile walk, stay on my T factor low-fat diet, have lost twenty pounds, and most important keep up with my index options trading. I have made $110,000 since December. Mr. Hunt. It is all mock trading you understand, but someday it will be real. As soon as I can come up with $10,000 bucks to open a real account. There are plenty of *Wall Street* journals around so we can keep track of the market. Mr. Hunt is a millionaire many times over. He had a radio show in Miami. So from now on, it is diamond rings, cadillacs, and cocktails by the pool! Mr. Hunt and I have become walking partners. It is less boring when you have someone to talk to. He was locked up with Crazy Eddie before he came here. His prices are insane!

I go outside all the time here, not like Westmoreland. There are no fences at all. People walk away all the time now that the weather is mild. They have volleyball, softball, racket ball, bocci ball, etc. It's by the balls they get you!

"Big-legged woman keep your dresses down. You got somethin' up under there. Make a bulldog hug a hound!"

Whatever I do, it's got to be funky.

Still chillin' with the rest of the villains.

Love,
Mel

Dear Charlene,

Thank you for the angel postcards. They are beautiful. I have them both hanging up around the picture of Neb that you sent. It reminds me that he is with the angels. Yes, I would love it if you sent me some more. I want to give one to my friend Mr. Hunt. He is a spiritual man in a more structured way.

I am working on trying to get the kids down for a visit. I don't think that Lynn M. will bring them. Jim M. says he doesn't want his kids to see him down here like this. Lynn may come down but not the kids. I will get them here somehow. I have about five pictures of you, also many great pics documenting some of the places we went with the kids, Bread & Puppet, Ben & Jerry, Edgar Cayce, and York Beach. I thank you for that.

Sorry to hear about your job situation. This resurgence of conservatism is everywhere. The BOP is pissed that they are supposed to be giving us time off for doing the drug program, so they are dragging their feet.

I am sorry if I hurt you with what I wrote in those letters. I have no retort. I don't even remember a lot about those days. I was a jerk. I'd like to take a lot of things back. You are a special person. Sorry, I hurt you. Feel free to blast me any time.

Love,
George

Letter number 30, FPC Allenwood, April 1995 to Charlene Wakefield

Charlene,

It is an endless uphill battle with depression around here, boredom and depression. Some days I manage to get out of bed, and things go pretty well. I walk the track (three miles). I go to work. I am my usual self with a kind words for everyone, a positive attitude, trying to cheer up others who are losing their battle that day. At work, they call me the Nice Guy. I interact well with all races and creeds. I even get along with real criminals who have worked their way down from the FCIs. I say to myself, "George, you can do this. It is only time and space." The days keep whizzing by. My days off seem to come by so quickly. Then there are those other days. I have all that I can do to drag my ass out of bed. I don't want to talk to people, and I am surrounded by hundreds of them. I sleep as long as I can. I sleep till I can't sleep no more. I don't feel like exercising. I just want to die. Thanks you for the Urantia stuff and the angel postcard. I haven't read all of the info. I got an application to the conference in Hawaii. Not gonna make that conference. Thanks for writing and being my friend again.

George

Here is a test to see if your mission on Earth is finished.
If you are alive, it isn't!

Johnny Boy,

Well, I'm ready to come home. This sucks! Monday nothing, Tuesday nothing, and the beat go on. We saw *Interview with a Vampire* tonight. Travis sent me the book. I got some nice Father's Day cards yesterday. I actually got six letters, not including yours. One letter was from Susan with a copy of Neb's autopsy report. The cause of death was a brain aneurism. I handled it! Thanks for the picture of Marlene Dietrich. She was your favorite a few years back, was she not?

I got accepted into the drug program, and we are getting the year off for sure. I am going Monday to talk to the counselor and find out when I can start. Some friends graduated today and Weatherby has already completed it. Now we will be getting out around the same time. He wants to go to Florida, and I want to come home to the Green Mountains. Mom and Dad want me in Connecticut, but I need to be near the kids.

I got a letter from Owl today. He turned down some jobs. He doesn't know if he made the right move or not.

Jim M. and I are getting a bit closer. I never really got a chance to know him. He is an okay guy. He is having a harder time here than me. He is a short-timer and not as accepting of some things. You can't control the outside world and he tries to.

I am still losing weight. I had to turn in all of the clothes I got when I first got here. I'm gonna be a lean mean sex machine when I get out of here.

You look more like "Big Brad" (his father) in that picture every day.

Well, that's all the news from the *joint* for now. Be good, say your prayers, hang bail. Twenty years of schooling, and they put you on the day shift. Threw the bums a dime in your prime. Hard to tell if anything is gonna sell. Don't wanna be a bum you better chew gum. The pump doesn't work 'cause the vandals took the handles. Shut up. J. K., keep your feet still.

Love,
Melvin

Charlene,

I did learn something today that fills my mind with possibilities. I went to see my shrink who is in charge of the drug program here because I received notification of acceptance into the drug program. I was trying to get an idea as to when I would be starting. He told me that I was set to go but probably not till April of next year when I would be twenty-four months from my release date. However, unbeknownst to me, I am on the *national list* meaning that if they have an opening at another facility, and I agree to a transfer, I could start sooner. Everyone who I have spoken to says FCI Butner, North Carolina, is a sweet place to do time. Just as many say that it sucks. I would be with M. W. It is farther away than Vermont, but I don't get many visits anyway.

I got a letter from Lynn along with some excellent Father's Day cards. The kids are great. I finally got a letter from Grace. She flunked her driver's test because her mother wouldn't let her practice enough, and she couldn't go to the Grateful Dead concert for lack of funds. It made me sad but glad that she told me. I miss those kids.

I miss Nebadon so much. I was just reading my manual for making contact with the teachers (Urantia book). It was intense and mind-boggling. I am going to start trying to tune in. I am willing. I just hope that I can get myself into a quiet space within. They are entirely welcome to anything I have to offer. Take me, use me. I wonder if any of you folks have seen a young fellow named Nebadon Wesche up there. If so, tell him that I love him and miss him, and if he thinks of it, maybe on his day off, he could pop into my consciousness for a second, and say hello to his pop. I love the little saying at the end. "When we talk to the deity or celestial beings, society calls it prayer. When celestial beings talk to us, society calls it schizophrenia."

Well, gotta go for now. I am sleepy.

Take care,
George

El Monk (another alias),

You bad. Thanks for Rita. She be funky too! She's my favorite honky! I just saw Jim M. He is staring off into the visitor parking lot looking for his wife and kids. I hope he has a good visit. I could use one myself.

Things are going along about the same. The drug program starts in April of 1996. I will be home six to nine months after that. Time flies when you are having fun. It's windy here a lot, and it does make me nervous. Think I might stab someone after lunch for yuks. We had two intensely hot days, and then it got cool again. That's cool and the gang.

Speaking of cafeteria food, I'm still driving the soup bar. Soon I hope to be driving the salad bar. Same pay, fewer hours.

I haven't been able to watch TV lately because you need a radio with earphones to tune in to the stations. I ain't got no money honey for a radio. I have been rich, and I been poor, and rich is better.

It's Friday night, but I have to work tomorrow. My days off are Sunday and Monday.

Harrison is my roommate. He is twenty-nine and going on twenty-one. He was born in Nigeria. He came to this country I don't know when. I am the only white boy in my neighborhood. It's cool; I just terrorize all of the other minorities. I am the oldest by far, and Papa doesn't take no mess.

I am down to 230 pounds. I have forty pounds to go. I also want to gain ten pounds in my pecker. You know, to keep the girls happy! I am trading in my forty-six-inch pants for forty-two inches.

I got some nice birthday and Father's Day cards. Mom and Dad celebrated their fiftieth wedding anniversary. I was going to send them to England and Ireland. Instead, they had to send me $50.00. It will happen. I will be back.

Take care.
Mel

Johnny,

'Sup, brah. How has your summer been? We are having a heat wave. It's intense. Jeannie says it's a shocker. We all hang out on the patio till 3 p.m. and go under the hose just like when we were kids. I am off thank God for two days. The chow hall is too fucking hot.

I had another interview with the counselor who gets you into the drug program. He asked me a bunch of questions about my drug use. I melted his pen for him!

I am set to go into the class in April. Nine months from then into a halfway house. Home in eighteen months. Time flies when you are having fun!

Tomorrow is July 17, my second wedding anniversary. I haven't heard from Viola since June 6th, her birthday. Boy, I can't wait to see her. 'Cause I'm ready, ready as anybody can be. I'm ready for love. I hope she's ready for me.

I got a letter from Mike W. We will be released around the same time. I can't wait for eighteen months. Hell, I miss everybody.

I have to write a bunch of letters tonight. I have been putting it off now for days because of the heat. My cousin sent me three books, and the post office didn't cancel the stamps. Jackpot! It's the little things. I got five freebies. So this letter is getting a free ride son!

Be cool.

Write soon.

Mel

Letter number 35, FPC, Allenwood, July 21, 1995

El Monk (another alias),

Well, that last letter was *Classic Kravetz*. It said nothing and everything at the same time.

Well, it finally happened. In spite of myself, I have found a positive addiction. I have to walk every day for an hour. It is about four and a half miles. And for the first time since high school, I played tennis. I had a great time, sweated like a pig, didn't get too winded, and actually won two games. I have decided to become addicted to tennis. So I have dedicated the rest of the summer to the game. Still losing weight.

I spoke to Viola on July 17, our second wedding anniversary. She is still waiting. I can't wait for some of that Dominican loving. *Mucho gusto*. They call me El Magnifico. Sort of like El Monk but not as intense!

I got a new job now. Instead of driving the soup bar, I am driving the salad bar. I can play tennis the rest of the day. So when I get out we should play. The babes love tennis bums too.

I am about to get a single cube (living quarters). A guy from Shelton, Connecticut, who went to high school with Monk is leaving, and I am in line for his single cube.

My friend Brian B. from *Unsolved Mysteries* got twelve years and seven months from the same judge who sentenced me. They are supposed to be changing the guidelines in September. He is in Rutland right now. I hope he comes here soon.

That's about it from this end, dude. It is late, and I can't sleep even though I walked five miles and played tennis for two hours and didn't have my nap. I must be getting stronger.

See ya, dude.

Love,
Mel

Hi, Charlene,

Sorry I haven't written in a while. It has been hot and nothing much has happened. The BPO likes it that way.

I got the letter from Mike. Thank you.

Mort had a *Valley Times Journal* (hometown paper). They had lots of pictures of Alumni Weekend and also the Saxtons River July 4th celebration. I saw the new pavilion and some of the floats. I miss Vermont.

I'm still waiting for the drug program. I can't wait to start doing this stuff. Most guys I talk to have only good things to say. It can really give you a lot of answers, also guidance about being reintroduced to the kids. That's something that I think a lot about. I spoke to Travis a few weeks ago, and he told me that he was mad. You can't blame him. He had a hell of a time. I feel very guilty about how I screwed him and his sister up. A lot of the DP has to do with family relations.

I asked Grace if she would be interested in working at Harlow's. I got no response. Travis got a job as a teacher's aide, $125.00 a week. He makes more than me.

And their mom, I can't believe she just does nothing. I told Travis how proud I was of him.

I got a card today from Susan with pictures of Neb's grave site, also pics of the bench.

Well it's time to go call the kids.

Take care,
George

Letter number 37, FPC Allenwood, August 9, 1995

Johnny,

"Don't say I don't love you 'cause I don't ever treat you right. You know I'm a country boy. I just love to stay out all night."

And now a moment of silence for the passing of a truly legendary freak and guitar player extraordinaire, the leader of the Grateful Dead, Jerry Garcia. He will be missed. It's a miracle he lived this long. The boy loved to party. We should dry him out and smoke him! Happy trails, Jerry. I had a pint of Cherry Garcia in toast to the man. I can't believe he is gone. I listened to some Dead music on the radio and watched a couple of tributes on the tube. Carlos Santana said he feels a loss. Many questions arise. Owl sent me a subscription to Rolling Stone. The next issue should be all "Dead." What will happen to the little amp? Will they go on? It is a sad day for rock 'n' roll.

I just got a letter from Bugaboo. He and Owl will be down for visit on August 17th. Hop in the car dude. Make my year. Don't worry. I will be home!

Love,
Miro

Hello, love,

They are starting to release all of the guys who completed the drug program. There are about one hundred guys leaving any day now. More room for me.

Kravetz Bugs and Owl were here Saturday for a visit. It was a great visit, and I hated to see them leave. I was depressed for a day or two, but I am better now. I even got a nice card from Susan. I also got a postcard from Willy.

I am getting very high on this Urantia book literature. Reading it is mind-expanding. I wish I could get my U book in here. I talked to the chaplain, and he said that the BOP has this lame rule about books with hard covers unless they are ordered from the publishers. It seems kind of a waste to order another one when I have a perfectly good one at home. I could read one paper a day and read the whole book before I got out.

The chaplain is kind of a straight local guy. There used to be a town here when the feds bought it. They raised the town and only left this beautiful old chapel to make way for the prison complex. We walk down to it every day. I finally went inside. It is beautiful.

When Kravetz was here, I told him about Beth M. Gracie told me she had full-blown AIDS. My question to him was when was the last time he made love to Mary S. Because Dave D. who is sometimes with Mary used to screw Beth all the time. At least that is what he said. He is the biggest liar I have ever met.

That is really good news about "No Smoking" in Rita's Diner. I never would have believed it. Used to be you couldn't see across the room. I can't wait to get myself one of their greasy burgers! The ones we get here are low-grade dog food. I also miss the velvet paintings. They were just the touch.

I just went through all of my paperwork dealing with this place. I can't find your visit approval but I'm sure you are on the list. You could call and find out. I'd love to see you. Wear something with cleavage. I'm flirting again.

That's all folks.

G

Johnny Mon,

Here is your photo. You look like Bill Kreutzmann. The Lettuce Brothers live in the big house! Bad news, Angelo had the camera strap over his lens so we only got two good shots. Dennis and Nancy were here today. I had a shot taken with them too. We had a good visit. They bought me a roast beef sandwich and ice cream then jumped in the car and headed back to the Green Mountains.

Looking for some songs to play? Here is some music trivia for you. For three free strings at the Bowlero and a box of fries (heavy ketchup), what recently decided keyboard man wrote "Don't put no headstone on my grave" and "Who will the next fool be"? The answer will be in the next letter.

Rolling Stone outdid themselves with their latest issue about Jerry and the Dead. It was the truth. Wouldn't tell you no lies!

I just traded in my forty-two-inch pants for a size forty inches. I lost four pounds in two weeks, 224 pounds and falling. I entered the Columbus Day tennis tournament. Mel (love) Miro, tennis' new bad boy, we're gonna kick your ass.

Still no rain down here. The place is gonna dry up and blow away. I hope it does. "Blow wind blow wind, blow my baby back home to me!"

See ya. wish I could be with ya.

Miro

Kravetz,

Another letter right on time. Thanks for the picture of fucking Owl. But you aren't the only one with good pictures. See if you can guess what this photo is of (Seaside Park in Bridgeport, Connecticut) For a $10.00 gift certificate to *Gifts from the Sea*, identify this place. No par in this place. Speaking of Florida, "Jula," Bugs, and Grace are headed to Florida. I told them to say hi to Godzilla in the sewer. Also watch out for sun damage.

I will identify the photo in my next letter.

Today I discovered a game that is much better than tennis. It is a racquetball. I am gearing my exercise program to indoor sports before it gets too cold. It is very windy, and you have to know that makes me nervous. Today I went crazy. I played two and a half sets of tennis (rained out), did thirty minutes on the stair stepper, and played racket ball for two hours. I will sleep tonight.

Did you know that Ola Tunji played at the memorial service in Golden Gate Park for Jerry Garcia? Well, now you do.

I gotta go stand in line for a phone so I can call the kids. It has been a while. Keep on writing. I look forward to the letters…

Mel

Johnny,

Sorry to hear about your IRS troubles. Those fucking Nazis. I say burn the flag! I am so fucking bored. I can't stand it.

I just got a letter from Mike W. He got a year off of his sentence for doing the drug program. I can't wait to get started. Only eighteen or nineteen months to go. April I start.

Today I played tennis and went on the stair stepper. I burned 575 calories in 35 minutes. Tomorrow will be more of the same. I can't wait to get out of food service. You only have to stay at a job for three months. I have been there for over nine months. They won't let me out. Institutional need they say. I don't get to go to the greenhouse. The only other alternative is medical. I will find out tomorrow.

I am waiting for them to clear the count so I can go take a big crap.

See you later.

Love,
Miro

Brother Luke,

I am out of food service. Free Mel and OJ lol. No longer am I the salad person. Now I work in the recreational dept. Don't know what I will be doing, but it has got to be better. I was getting into a rut. I will find out tomorrow. I can spend my whole day working out. Guys don't work very long in rec. Usually about a half-hour a day. Some work longer. I got a great picture of the Bug man himself. He is getting gray as we all are.

Nice picture of crystal Healing Soonta. Crazy Billy just dropped by to borrow some coffee. I forgot to ask him that question, but suffice it to say that cultivation is not the biz to be in for the nineties. They would love to lock your hippie ass up. It gives them a boner! I just came back from Chow. Billy said he had 468 plants (second beef), but I know guys in here for a lots less. I am expecting Russel M. any day now (thirty-four months for conspiracy).

Today was my first day in recreation. I went on the stair master from ten to eleven, had lunch, checked in at twelve thirty, and was told that I won't be assigned to a job until Saturday. I am not supposed to show up on Saturday. My friend George Bushey (we always answer each other's pages when they call us over the PA system), only works on Saturday and Sunday. He covers and uncovers the pool tables. The rest of the week he does nothing. I can't wait to find out what I will be doing. I am buying some racquetballs today. I will show you how to play. We can practice down at the Gentle Bud Memorial Field.

I have been thinking about growing a beard. Maybe I will shave my head and face and let them grow in at the same length. I would look like a Chia Pet!

That's about it for this letter. I think I will go shoot some pool.

Love,
Miro

Kravetz,

> All the girls turn the color,
> Of an avocado,
> When he drives down the street,
> In his El Dorado,
> He was only five feet three,
> The girls could not resist his stare.
> Nobody ever called Pablo Picasso an asshole,
> Not like you/not in New York.

Ask Angelo who did that song. FYI, the butthole surfers did it in *Repo Man*. There's some music trivia for you.

Last night, the Yankees lost a squeaker to Seattle. This place is loaded with Puerto Rican "Yankee" fans. They went crazy, and one pulled the fire alarm. It was also the full moon. At 2 a.m., they had us outside standing for an hour. Fuckin' peckerheads!

I showed up for my new job today, and the boss saw me for the first time. He has seventy guys and forty jobs so everyone works a half-hour a day. He gave me a job on Saturday and Sunday for about an hour. I have to sweep and mop the pottery studio and the exercise room. Monday thru Friday I have off. I now make $6.50 a week. My mother said she would send me some dollars, plus I have some cash stashed with Dennis and Nancy. I spend less than $20.00 a month. All I buy is stamps.

I have plenty of time to work out now. I spent forty-five minutes on the Life Step then I walked three miles. I played tennis all afternoon, came back to my cube, and fell asleep.

Lynn sent me a letter telling me about you going sailing with Jim and Nora. Bugs and Grace are going to Florida, cool. I am growing a beard to celebrate being liberated from the kitchen. God, this place is boring!

I just got a letter from you, Will Corbet, Slappy, and my friend Brian, the guy I was locked up with in New Hampshire. You remember he was on *Unsolved Mysteries*? I can't believe it. He got twelve years and seven months. He filed a double jeopardy motion, and he won! He is out in Cornish, New Hampshire, with his girlfriend. The feds have thirty days to appeal. That's good news. He didn't deserve the shit he got. He should sue. He was in jail for two and a half years.

Thanks for the art.

Love,
Miro

Charlene,

Undoubtedly you have heard of the nationwide Federal Prison Lockdown going on right now. We are just about the only place that is functioning normally. The other three facilities here are all locked down so the guys from here who work there here have had a few days off. Some of our guys have had to go over to the penitentiary and make sandwiches for 22,000 inmates. They torched the whole kitchen. It's a nationwide protest, and I am in sympathy with them. It's the crack dealers, and they are protesting the fucking they just got which will be voted into law on November 1st. It is a law that reduces the penalty for pot plants from one kilo per plant to one hundred grams which will let out all the white pot growers. The motion to make crack quantities equal to white powder quantities was voted down. So, all of the black street dealers have nothing coming.

There is a guy in here doing ten years for two ounces of crack and they got me with over a pound of powder. I only got sixty-three months with eighteen months off for doing the drug program. Even though they found all the stuff to make free base in my possession, thank God that meant nothing. The brothers are pissed, and I don't blame them.

Seven different prisons went off. We had two fires started in our unit. One place in Florida was burned pretty badly. They are having a big investigation here. What a racist low. I'm glad it won't affect me, but those crack kids deserve a break too.

Also, I hear that I may qualify for a two-point reduction clause for a nonviolent first offender, no weapons, no king pinpoints. I could get a year off. I have to talk to one of the lawyers in here and believe me there are plenty. They all hate the feds which are more than I can say for some people's representation. Lots of guys paid a lot of money to lawyers before they realized that when you go up against the feds, you can't win.

I got my Harley back because they took it from Dennis's and Nancy's house. That is a no-no.

Unsolved Mysteries wants to settle out of court since they aired Brian's story, and he was acquitted, $10 million, defamation of character. You go, Brian B. That is not enough. He is at his mom's house on Long Island under house arrest pending the decision to appeal by the feds. They have till November 6th to decide whether they will let him go or contest the decision.

Keanu Reeves is gay. He is secretly having an affair with Tom Cruise. It is true. I read it in *Weekly World News* right next to the article "Man forces dog to smoke cigarettes" and the picture of Bill Clinton with a space alien.

Well, I gotta go now love. Thanks for the letters they really help. I love you.

George

Inmates are not allowed to correspond with each other so I had to send this letter to a mutual friend who interns forwarded it to Mike

Mikey,

Hey, dude. What's happening? Not a lot I bet. It's Halloween weekend, and we are having a film festival. Only thing is all the films are lame horror flicks. Yesterday they showed Bram Stoker's *Dracula*. I remember going to see it with Charlene at the Latches and falling asleep. I thought it was probably because I had been up for a few days but I fell asleep again. Today is *Needful Things*. That was a cool movie.

FPC Allenwood is in the process of expanding the drug program. The goal is to have 150 white-collar inmates here to run the camp and have the whole place become a drug rehab. I am still set to start on April 1, 1996. They caught two guys cheating and threw them out. Then they let them back in. I think it will be a little more relaxed over there now that it is expanding. They had a mad rush there for a while when it was first announced about the year off. It was harder to get in, but now they have more money for classes, and they definitely want it full. More money for them.

Big troubles down the road at the FCI. Inmates trashed food service and guys from here volunteered to go make sandwiches (twelve-hour shifts). Fucking scabs. Let the hacks do the work. A truckload of trashed new carpets came by headed for the dump. No inmates on the truck just hack. All of the other guys that work at the other joints have been off for two weeks.

I am working in recreation now. I spend my day exercising.

I got a letter from Slappy the other day. They are fine. My kids and Will C. write often. I love the letters.

Take it easy, bro. The nightmare is almost over for both of us.

George

El Monk,

Well, they are still locked down over at the prison complex. They tried to let them out a couple of times, but the place just went off again. Guys from here that work over there will be getting another week off. Travis told me that Mike W. has been locked down in his cell for two weeks. He is in an FCI which is a maximum-security prison. All of those guys are locked down nationwide.

But I just keep on keeping on with my program: working on my exercise program and trying to get healthy. I think they just voted to remove free weights from all facilities. They say that they can be used as weapons. The inmates say that guards are intimidated by some of these bodybuilders. The screws have their own weight room, so why don't they use it? That is going to piss off a lot of guys. Weight training is a lifestyle in prison. People in here live for that. Personally I don't get it but when there is very little to do people tend to get into things more.

There she is again,
Standing over the record machine
Looking like a model,
on the cover of a magazine.
She's too cute,
To be a minute over seventeen!
Go, go little queenie!

I got a letter and a check from my land partner Paul in Toronto. He didn't forget me. His wife and Viola are good friends. It's good to know that I can count on him. We could both be rich someday if they ever get that airport built. I will be rolling in pesos. Gonna get myself a new low rider with furry dice and have *merengue diablo* painted on the side!

A moment of silence for Alison Steele, the Nightbird… She will be missed.

A bunch of pot growers are going home. They got retroactivity and quantity reduction. Lots of guys can get out. They may have given guys with twenty-six criminal points, criminal category 1, first offense. No organizing points, a two-point reduction. So I may be eligible for something.

Travis told me that Russel M. is coming here. I will be on the lookout for him.

Well, Krav, it is time for lunch.

Love,
Miro

Letter number 47, FPC Allenwood, November 14, 1995, to Charlene Wakefield.

On or about November 6, 1995, I received a letter from the Vermont State Police. They were interested to see if I had any information about a drug-related murder that took place in our area a few years earlier. Enclosed please find a copy.

Dear Charlene,

What do you think of that letter? And you thought this was gonna be another dull letter! Who the hell is Walt J.? Probably someone I sold coke to in one of my stupors. That's what I get for babbling, I guess. I don't have any information about who killed her. I didn't even know her. That was pretty intense. I wrote them back and told them that I knew nothing. If I did have any information I would have gladly volunteered it.

Well, the asshole doctors here misdiagnosed a friend of mine's x-rays and told him that his arm was arthritic. It was a malignant tumor, and Carl is going to lose their arm. They are sending him to a prison hospital in Rochester, Minnesota. That is where the Mayo Clinic is. They want the specialists to see if they can save the arm. Big lawsuit if they can't. They get sued a lot.

So you were a flasher for Halloween! Did you tie a pepperoni to your fly as Raymond did in _Pink Flamingoes_?

Your paintings are gorgeous. The vineyard is my second favorite. My first favorite is the one you did at Stephen King's house. Remember that day we went to take pictures of the place, and SK came out to get the mail?

Speaking of _Unsolved Mysteries_, I called Marilyn B. the other night. (Brian B's girlfriend) to find out whether the feds were going to let him go or proceed with an appeal. (They had thirty days). Well, Marilyn picked up the phone and said, "George, I have someone here who wants to talk to you." It was Brian B. It was great to finally talk to him after a year. Turns out that after twenty-eight days, the feds filed another motion to the judge asking him to reconsider his ruling. The judge wrote a twenty-seven-page letter stating all of the reasons why he is letting Brian go. So the prosecution's motion is sour grapes. Brian has to notify his probation officer by giving his address. He is living on Long Island with his mom or he is up in Cornish, New Hampshire, with Marilyn. He is coming down for a visit.

Unsolved Mysteries was saying that Brian was a gambler, a gigolo, an international drug smuggler, and a heroin dealer, besides a pot grower which is really all that he was. When *Unsolved Mysteries* found out that the feds exaggerated the stories, they aired the show two more times. They were warned but did it anyway. Brian spoke to someone at U.M. and stated that the show makes so much money that they settle out of court for big bucks all the time. We shall see. Brian has a lawyer in New York City.

Dave S. is supposed to make halfway house this month. See what you can find out for me.

Love and kisses,
G.

Johnny,

Excellent cartoons you sent. I am tempted to post them on our bulletin board for all to see. I can't remember how many Veronica Lakes you sent. I think two.

Say a prayer for my son, Nebadon Wesche. He would have been nineteen years old on November 18, 1995. RIP.

James Brown got arrested again for smacking his wife, Adrien. Lawyers said it was just another episode in the continuing saga. He should dump that bitch and pick up with that foxy oriental babe that dances with him. I know I would!

It's snowing like a mofo here. We just lost power, and when that happens, all of the alarms go off. Everyone is afraid that they are going to make us go outside. Fuck it. I ain't going. Last night someone pulled the fire alarm as a distraction and took off. (Over the hill). They had an escape. At the same time, someone threw human shit on a guy's bed right next to my cube. The guy whose bed got hit was working overtime, and the turd sat there for hours. Then because of the escape, we had a count, and they kept us in here with the *turd* for an hour. "Get down."

"You got to be funky!" So everyone opened the windows, and we all froze. I slept in my coat. I hope they catch the moron who put the *turd* in Frank's bed! That's sick.

I played four games of racquetball today. I won them all. We are bad! Actually they are not good! I got a job switch here, now I keep the pool room clean. Every once in a while, I make sure no one threw anything on the floor. I am spending the winter in the gym.

Happy birthday, Big Brad, Johnny's father.

I may be getting a sentence reduction, a safety valve passed with a two-point reduction. I fall into fifty-four to sixty-three months instead of sixty-three to seventy-eight months which is where I sit now. Ten months, I'll take it. Well, bro. Keep in touch.

Love,
Melvin

Letter number 49, FPC Allenwood to John Kravetz, November 24, 1995

Johnny,

They never canceled your stamp, so this letter is free. Thanksgiving was a real food fest. They gave us tons of food. I kept close to my diet, but I had a good meal.

I was having lunch. I looked over, and Russel M. was sitting next to me. It was great to see him. We spent the rest of the day catching up on all the shit. He lives right down the hall from me. It is nice when someone from home shows up.

I am still set to go into the drug program in April, but if I get bumped till June, I will still get the eighteen months off. I am not worried especially because they are adding on three more classes.

Russel is trying to go to boot camp. If he completes it in six months, they will send him to a halfway house and then home.

Beth got sixty-three months and is doing it in Alderson, West Virginia. That is the same place where Big Daddy's friends (Leona and Mitch) from New York City, and Linda, Gary's wife the famous hash smuggler from Morocco, did some time. Also don't forget Martha Stewart did a little stretch there. And the river of shit flows on.

The child support people sent me a letter saying that I owe them $600, and they are going to dock my pay. I make $8.00 a month. They are welcome to it. I have written them three times stating that I am in jail. They never respond.

See ya and can't wait to be with ya!

M. M.

Kraveta,

December 1: my one-year anniversary here at Allenwood. Big fuckin' deal. This time next year I should be seeing the light at the end of the tunnel. Sagers is out and back on the couch at Sue's house. No halfway house and not required to get a job! Dogshit Dave.

Today we are having a gospel group from Baltimore come and give a concert. That should be pretty cool. All the way from Baltimore, "the Baltimore Baltimore." You dirty heuers! You still putting them things in your mouth? Ha cha cha! I was going to open a bakery, but I couldn't raise the dough. I was going to become a dentist, but I didn't have the patience. You should have been here last night. Some guy fucked a chicken! I'd like to see that. Gimmie that goddammed chicken! One more month, and it will be 1996. Great, keep 'em coming. Let's get on with this shit.

We don't get too many jokes in here. That's because this place is no joke.

I just got a letter from Stacy. She left Larry and now lives in Babe's trailer across from Twin Falls in Grangeville. Poor kid. What is going on in that hillbilly brain of hers?

Well, dude, keep those cards and letters coming. Me and Jeannie read them all.

Love,
Mel

El monk,

Did I say 214 pounds? Well, it's 213 pounds. Working out first thing every morning. Subtracting 1,200 calories a day. I feel pretty good.

It was terribly cold here for a couple of days. Today, it is 45 degrees and sunny. Not too much snow which pissed off the landscape guys because they couldn't use the snow blowers and had to shovel by hand. They were out shoveling all night. Sure am glad that I ain't on the snow shoveling team!

The gospel group was excellent with much *Brown Sugar*! Everyone got down. It was like Cleophus Brown in the Blues Brothers.

This weekend is a pool tournament which means more work for me. I may have to work an extra fifteen minutes. What the fuck man! Prison reform now! "Free Mel." Your brother is in chains. They interrupted my workout. Where is the justice?

I haven't seen much football although it is on constantly. Tonight is the Tyson fight, so you won't be able to get into the TV room. The brothers rule when it comes to sports. There's talk of removing the tennis courts, but they put outdoor lights so the brothers can play basketball outdoors at night.

I went to the dentist today. I have one cavity. I haven't had one in many years. They have an excellent dental plan. It's free. Did you get my Christmas card?

I finally got a letter from Duke. He is retiring and moving to Florida. Cool. Please send me his address. It was good to finally hear from him.

Things are progressing along as usual. Christmas is coming right up which is good so that it can be over. The new year 1996. I am out in 1997.

I just got some nice pics of Grace and Travis. I bought frames. I put them on my desk with pictures of Viola. I talked to her last week.

She can't wait for her "El Magnifico" (*con pinga grande*) to return! "El Magnifico" can't wait either.

I am hoping to get some time off for that safety valve thing. But chances are slim to none, and Slim is out of town.

Love,
Miro

Charlene,

Jimmy C. says thanks for the cards. The angel is great. We all love it.

I'm hoping for a halfway house in Southern Vermont. Right now there are only ones in Rutland, St. Johnsbury, Woodstock, and Burlington. If I finish the drug program I have to spend six months in one of those places. They need one in Southern Vermont.

My counselor asked me where I wanted to go when my time is up. I told him that I was homeless. I have eighteen months to figure that out.

I don't know if the new gun law will help Beau and Tuba. They were enhanced because guns were in the house or car, even if they were not used in the commission of a crime. Beau was wearing him to a dope deal. I don't know if they have a case.

It just stopped snowing here after depositing eighteen inches. It was beautiful, but lots of guys were on snow removal crews, and they were shoveling all night. Russel runs a snow blower. Yes, Russel is Beth's brother. They never caught him with anything, but he got thirty-three months. Beth and Mike D. ratted him out. He is going to be okay. He got into the drug program and will start in January. Nice guy, but really got screwed. If they want you they will get you right or wrong.

"'Good art doesn't match your couch.' I like that!"

A moment of silence for Jr. Walker "Shotgun." He will be missed. Take care, love. Write soon.

George

Take it easy, Nicky. He didn't mean it.

Knock it off. Cut that out, you knucklehead. I mean it.

The government is going out of business. They tried not to pay us. Tried to say that we were nonessential, but it is not true. This place cannot run without us, so they cut our pay in half and we get our full pay once this whole shit thing blows over. Just remember, you gotta wash your ass. Not the whole ass, the asshole! Words of wisdom. So this month I get $4.00 instead of $8.00. I used to make $23.00 a month, and I worked my ass off. And so for $8.00, I sit on my butt. And yes I am still working out. I got a new job. I go in at 8 a.m. and take the covers off the pool tables Monday to Friday. That's Bug's dream job. Running a pool hall. No beer, no food, no broads, no booze, no candy. Just straight pool.

So Brother Brown lost his wife Adrien this week. Sorry, James. You are still the godfather.

It snowed eighteen inches here. The poor bastards here have to go shoveling at 3 a.m. Everyone tries to get out of it and that pisses off the hacks so they start writing *shots*. Everyone gets into shit except Mello Bill Miro who uncovers the pool tables. Then I work out all day. I need a marathon pussy-eating extravaganza!

People really like the bulletin board I started with all the stuff you send.

Well that's all for now.

Love and kisses,
Miro

Letter number 54, FPC Allenwood, January 14, 1996, to John Kravetz

Johnny,

Our letters must have crossed in the mail. I got letters from Slappy, Charlene, Will Corbet, and Staci all on the same day. Staci split up with Larry. He got his fourth and fifth DWIs and is going to jail. That girl has a thing for us jailbirds.

Ladies love outlaws like babies love stray dogs.

Ladies touch babies like a miner touches gold.

Outlaws, they touch ladies somewhere deep down in their souls. I said that.

We are having another three-day weekend, Martin Luther King's birthday. Lots of movies and pool tournaments. I am in my cube reading and sleeping. It's football playoff. I will probably watch later on. Go, Giants.

We just had to count. Now it is time for lunch. Then who knows. The sun is out, so maybe I'll go for a walk. My good pen just ran out of ink. They sell really shitty ones in this place. I'm gonna have to steal a good one.

Sharon was approved for my visiting list. I hope they come visit soon.

News flash: "Mr. and Mrs. America and all the ships at sea." The Supreme Court is hearing a double jeopardy rule to see if it is constitutional. If it is shot down, my friend Brian will be coming to jail.

MM

El Monk,

Excellent blowup of Howlin' Wolf and company. I will be sending you some other priceless shots I have come across in my travels, not that I travel at all! Send them back, and I will post them on the Band News bulletin board down in the recreation room. People seem to enjoy them. I know they gonna love this one. That's an old shot of H. W. back before he was "Built for comfort, I ain't built for speed. But I got everything a young girl needs!"

My friend Guitar Billy went to my boss and said that the rehearsal room was disgusting and that if he hired Billy, he would be in charge of keeping it clean. The boss went for it, and Billy and I cleaned it out. We found two slide trombones, a bugle, two trumpets, and two saxophones laying around with two amplifiers, also mike stands and two conga drums. We can start a _merengue_ band.

Christmas is a sad time in jail. No one wants to be reminded that they will be away from family and friends, but New Year is always great. It marks the passing of another year and closer to the door. Now I can say that I will be out next year, 1997. So I got that going for me.

Lynn says she will bring the kids down to see me on spring vacation. That will be my Christmas present.

Well, that is about all for now. Keep on keepin' on.

Miro

El Monk,

I just got off the stair master. An hour a day keeps the pounds away. So Saturday I step into the blues, a blues band in the rehearsal room that is. "I am the groan of dying men." Guitar Billy practices in the broom closet, strange boy, health freak, musician type, clean living, tree-hugging individual. He steals food from the cafeteria to feed our stray cats. Some faggot hack kicked one of our cats the other day. Everyone said it was because he doesn't like pussy! He likes to check out peckers though. He is a *pecker checker* (he he)! Two guys got sent to the *hole* last night for sneaking in a package from the street. They were set up and swatted. Swatted like fleas. That's flies!

I got a letter from my friend Brian. He is the guy who got out on a double jeopardy ruling. They are appealing his win to the Supreme Court. They are hearing two test cases and will render a decision in April. If it is denied, Brian will have to come back to jail. I think that if I were him I would bolt. He has no kids, and he knows people all over the world. He was on the run for three and a half years already. Excellent dude.

A friend of mine, Norman, has just returned on a violation from Hartford Conn. halfway house. He was caught drinking. He said that place was such a pain in the ass that he should have stayed here. He is an alcoholic, and he owns a bar.

Well it's time for lunch, so I gotta go.

Love and kisses,
Mel Big House" Miro a.k.a. the Mighty Red Bastard, the Red Head

Johnny,

Great picture of Jr. Walker. This will make a great new addition to my bulletin board.

We had a knuckle check last night. There was a fight last night in the bathroom (pretty bad), and the guy who got beat won't rat on the guy who beat him so he went straight to the hole. Also, one of the Mafia guys had a going-away party, and during the night, they put honey in the locks of the counselor's offices, so they took away TV privileges for a week. I don't give a shit, but the young guys will suffer on the weekends.

Jim is trying to get another job back here. He is building housing for the screws, and he hates it. Everyone is fucking up, making the job take longer because the hacks who are in charge ($28.00 an hour) are never there. They want to milk it. He wants to get out before the shit hits the fan.

Slappy and Jean sent me some great books, one on Bill Haley that is intense. He also sent some gangster books. I am reading four books a week.

We had floods here, and some of the inmates have been going out to help the town's people. I was going to go, but they won't give me rain gear. I may go anyway just for something different to do. Maybe I can go help the girls at the local whore house. Yuk yuk. A friend of mine is going so he can mention it in his appeal. It is mostly shoveling mud out of people's houses. Gotta go.

Love,
Miro

Hi, Chuck,

It's late, and I can't sleep, probably because I took a two-hour siesta this afternoon. Of all the luck, the one night I wanted to watch we lost our privileges for a week. We had some misbehaving a while ago so we all get punished.

The president declared Pennsylvania a disaster area because of flooding so the inmates with community custody have been going out to assist flood victims. I haven't gone yet, but I may go this week-end. You just walk up to any house, knock on the door, and ask if they need help. The town is full of convicts, and felons running around free! No one is being searched coming back in. People are giving the guys beer and food. I don't know if I could handle all that freedom.

How to buy distressed real estate is the title of my new ACE course. A guy named Bill Lilly developed the course while here in jail. He is doing time for offering houses to people who had no down payments which Bill Clinton recently made illegal. I guess before if you did that, you were acting as a bank, and that is illegal. Don't fuck with the money. It's a federal beef. They take money seriously in America. So now we have convicts teaching convicts how to scam the public. It's the government's answer to rehabilitation. Anyway I am going to see what's up.

So my son Travis is an artist. The only way I would ever hear about it was the way I did. He never writes. I will have to tell my sister. She is an art teacher. She will be pleased. I will have to write him and have him draw me something. He may be an artist, but he ain't no writer!

They gave us bag lunches for the Super Bowl yesterday. That's the BOP's version of a tailgate party.

The day before we had a Latin orchestra come from New York City to play for us. They were intense. It was very enjoyable.

I am still working out each day. I found out that the reason why we got all those brand-new exercise bikes was because they were rejected by the prison because they had too many parts that could be taken off and used as weapons.

My friend Stevie (Goomba coke dealer from Jersey) went out to help flood victims. Some little old lady said that he was an angel for helping her move all her ruined furniture. "Where are you from?" she asked.

"Saint Allenwood," he answered

"Where is that?" she asked.

"Federal Prison Camp." She flipped out. Then he said to her, "If you think they are doing such a good job moving stuff now, you should see them after dark with the furniture that is in good shape." She was not impressed.

My friend Billy Carvel is the only person who is legally allowed to smoke pot for medicinal purposes. They didn't give him any time off yet. Our resident inmate lawyer is working on sentence reduction.

Billy is way out there. Nice guy.

Love,
George

Shonny,

Today we had a special musical treat for our Latin brothers in chains, and I am still bleeding from the head stem! Van Lester *y sol orchestra*. Intense, intense, intense! They came all the way from New York City, keyboard, three trumpets, two trombones, congas, timbales, bongos, and other percussions, and Van on vocals. Look out, strange cat people. I am still reeling. The whole place went wild. It was a nice shot in the arm.

My ex-brother-in-law Billy died of pancreatic cancer. There is another kick in the ass. I always liked Bill. The last time I saw him was when Angelo and I went to visit him. I dropped Angelo off in Roswell, New Mexico, and stayed with him for about a week. His daughter, Emily, and Sarah must be pretty upset.

Viola sent me an electronic musical Valentine card, and they won't let me have it because they would have to destroy it to inspect it. fucking pig-pokin', dick-smokin', ball-bustin', rim-jobin', corn-cobin', goat-ropin', scrotum-lickin', hum-jobin' pencil neck geeks, and I say that with all due respect.

Well, I gotta go read my *People Magazine* that Bugman sent me. Michael Jackson and Lisa Marie Presley split up. Inquiring minds want to know.

I got a letter from Owl. He has the blues. The letter was pretty funny.

Love,
Miro

Charlene,

Look for a red pen. That is the most exciting thing to happen to me today. Thanks for the books. Jean sent me five gangster books a couple of days ago. I have plenty to read.

I started reading *Hoffa*. It is slow and dry and long.

My roommate John is from Waterville, Maine. He knows where the *Foot* was based when Slappy and I were up there. John is reading *Meyer Lansky*. I want to read that next. I just finished the autobiography of Marlon Brando. That was very good. He got more ass than a toilet seat.

Russel's wife Teri and Staci are coming in March. Staci is not on my visiting list, so I don't know if I will see her. She will be going to FCI Lewisburg to see her husband. Glen and Sharon were supposed to come that same weekend, but they changed to March 30th.

March is going to be intense. Gracie's birthday is March 3rd, and that is the anniversary of my son Nebadon's death. My sister's birthday is March 5th. I hope I get those visits to cheer me up. I like this pen.

I finally got my Urantia book calendar. The quotes are very inspiring.

My distressed real estate class is very interesting. There are lots of ways to acquire property. They actually get you started. You can also get money to fix up and live in these houses. It is a twelve-week course. There are a lot of talented people here. I think Jim is learning credit card fraud. Just kidding! I think.

I don't think that my septum will ever be the same. A doctor at FCI Otisville said that I don't need a septum. Mine is gone, too much cocaine went up there. The best part is I never get a stuffed-up nose. I was afraid of getting infections, but none so far.

No computers are allowed in here. The feds are too uptight. Some of the guys in here invented computers. Not even beginner classes. *No.*

Mike W. said that he may be coming to Boston for halfway house. He has a brother there. Some Vermont guys went there and some to Rutland, Vermont. I could take Boston for a while.

Sometimes I lay awake trying to figure a way to get the money I would need to take care of the kids. Starting over at fifty years old is scary. All I can offer is a sober father which is substantial, but in America, you need cash. I was thinking of staying in Boston for a year or so to try and make some money. I always wanted to live in a big city.

Anyway, as long as I get into the drug program by July/August, I will be halfway someplace in April 1997, thirteen months away. I can't believe it. Time drags when you are miserable.

Gotta go. Thanks for the letters.

G

El Monk,

"Screamin' and cryin'. Thinking 'bout my past love that's gone. She's a brown-skinned woman, but I love her just the same."

It's snowing like a mofo at camp what the fucks it to ya!

Charlene was supposed to visit tomorrow mofo but I am not too hopeful. We are supposed to get twelve inches. That's what she said. I almost lost my tit job. There were too many guys on the detail, so they took a pile off and put them in food service. I was having nightmares but so far so good. I am still opening the pool hall every weekday morning. Then I jump on the stair stepper (torture rack). Then off to the racquetball court. It's a tuff life.

I called the kids last night. It was Gracie's birthday. Staci came down last weekend. It was fun. Bugs and Grace will be here on March 30, I hope.

They are throwing people out of the drug program for gun enhancements. Thanks again to Staci for coming to my place and taking those pistols out of my nightstand and dresser drawers. "I was just trying to see what she brought me from Santa Clause." Four guys got thrown out today. The feds are trying to keep the population up. After all, that's how they get paid. This puts me closer to getting in. Once I am in, I can gauge better when I am leaving the *Rock*!

I was watching a show with astrologers. They were saying that Pisces women are coming out of two and a half years of problems with their children. Susan is a Pisces, and she lost a son. So things are looking up for the fish. Gracie has a nice boyfriend named Matt. He bought her a stuffed toy for her birthday. I am happy for her.

Thursday is my favorite day. We get two *Seinfeld's*. It is guaranteed laughs, something in short supply around here.

Viola sent me a Richard Bach book. The only problem is it is in Spanish. I ordered a copy in English from the library.

The picture of Chick Webb you sent will make an excellent addition to my bulletin board which now contains Jr. Walker and Howlin' Wolf. Let's see what else: diamond rings and watches.

That's it for now, brother.

Love and kisses,
The fabulous Moola

Otis,

'Sup, blood. Thanks for the pics of drummers. They will make an excellent addition to the bulletin board. Chick Webb was a big hit.

I guess I am going to keep my job in recreation. I survived the cut so far anyway. The big news is I am down to 200 pounds. Going strong and headed for 190 pounds. I am cutting back on the stair master and walking more. Today was sunny and 50 degrees. And tomorrow will be 60 degrees.

Maybe I will get a visit this weekend. She had to cancel last weekend because of snow. Tom and Rainey are supposed to come and visit Jim. It would be great to all be in the visiting room at the same time.

What do you get when you put fifty lesbians and fifty corrections officers in the same room together? One hundred people who don't do *dick*!

So Dave is moving out of my house. That will make the kids happy. Makes me happy too, fucking leach! It's time to start growing on someone else. Maybe we should introduce him to Kathy V. (the growth).

We got a new warden today. He came from FCI Otisville. I remember him from when I was there. We don't know what kind of a warden he will be yet. When you try to talk to him, his head keeps shaking no. There are lots of power struggles going on right now with the different factions.

Tomorrow I actually have to work. Rug shampooing day. The last time we did it I held an electrical and watched MTV. It took two hours. We should be done before lunch.

I played racquetball today with my Goomba friend Tony from Brooklyn. He went to UB and Southern same time as me.

Well, that's all folks. No siesta for me today, so I am gonna turn in early.

Miro

Letter number 62, FPC Allenwood, March 1996, to Charlene Wakefield

Dear Charlene,

It is Friday night, and I sort of halfway expect a visit from Bugs and Grace. They said they would be here on March 30th, tomorrow. That would be fun. We had an ice storm last night, but today is fine. Just came from a mail call but nothing for me. Your book will come next week.

High school class reunions. It could be fun except I am still in touch with my high school friends, Bugs, Grace, Owl, and Kravetz. I don't think I would like to see people I don't care about and listen to them bullshit me about how well they are doing.

So, there is another Charlene Wakefield in America. She couldn't be as sexy as you, my dear. Yes, we were the talk of the visiting room last weekend. Mr. Hunt noticed and passed a comment a few days later. But he wasn't the only one. We were a scandal!

Funny story: Charlene weighs ninety-nine pounds, and I asked her to smuggle me in an old and favorite pair of tennis shoes. They were a Jack Purcell model, a professional tennis player, hence the name Tennis Shoe. He was the first athlete to lend his name to a sneaker company. Charlene is so tiny that she was able to wear them over her regular shoes. The cops didn't notice, but to some of us, she looked like Bozo the Clown walking in. We pulled it off. I took my crappy old sneakers off and put them in the trash, put on the Jack Percells, and no one was any the wiser. Also a corrections officer had to warn us about being too lovey-dovey. It was a great visit!

I am getting impatient to start the drug program. There are no ACE courses over the summer, so I am going to go to NA twice a week during the summer. It will look good on my record. I really don't want to do coke anymore. It definitely fucked up my life. The more I think about it, the more I can see what a handful I must have been for others at times. I wasn't ready to stop then, but now I know I am powerless against cocaine.

My friend Jimmy C. works in the laundry, and today he scored me a pair of army fatigue cargo pants. Lots of guys have them, but

I guess I must look too much like a white-collar criminal because I got mostly kakis. These pants are definitely used with some holes. They would make great shorts, but I would probably get busted for destroying government property. I know they won't let me take them with me when I leave. They are perfectly broken in with paint stains and everything.

Well, it is 10:30 a.m. Saturday morning, and still no Bugs and Grace. B and G just got here. B and G just left. What an excellent visit. They said hello.

Love,
George

'Sup, keed,

Well, Mr. and Mrs. Buggington popped in last weekend. We had a nice visit. It was good to see the geekster again. My sister is coming with my kids this month. That's the visit I am looking forward to. It has been over a year. There is a rumor that Viola is coming to Canada and getting permission to visit me here.

April 4th was the second year of incarceration for me. Time flies when you are miserable. Jail isn't bad; it just sucks.

Don't ask me why, but you are not allowed to send me packages. Take no more than five paperbacks and mail them in a large envelope. It has something to do with the space they have in the mail room for packages that must be opened. Sounds like bullshit to me, but that's the way it is. As for the Urantia book, there shouldn't be any problem because it is coming from the publisher. I am getting permission just in case.

We started a petition to get food service to provide fat-free salad dressing. I wrote it. Cool, huh!

I might be having my Lincoln picked up and sold for me. I could use the bucks. I just called Charlene to get some directions for the guy. He lives in Springfield, Massachusetts. The car is in Charlemont, Massachusetts.

I got a card yesterday from Mike W. He is trying to get here for the last part of his bit. We are both getting out around the same time. So we may finish this shit up together. The only thing that would make this place better is if you were here. Why don't you go out and catch a case? Just a small one; twelve or fourteen months, and we could be cubies!

Sounds like you have another maniac on your hands. Where do you find them? It's been a while. Remember when Christian flipped out at the gray house (a commune in southern Vermont) and when Tia's friend did too much acid, and got naked on our neighbor's lawn at the yellow house (another commune)? He was holding on to his pecker and calling it his lifeline. Ha ha! I think you are a magnet.

I just got a letter from my daughter with lots of pictures. I also got a letter from my sister saying that she is bringing the kids down for a visit. Two to three weeks!

I went over to see the director of the drug program. Dr. Findlay and pick up an NA book. (It turns out he wasn't really a doctor). Anyway, he said that it looks like I won't be getting into the program until October, so I won't be getting the full year off. Bummer. That sucks but what can I do. It is better than nothing.

Other than that, the river of shit flows on.

It's been snowing here the past few days. It's gonna snow again tonight. The Canadian geese are returning, and it will soon be beautiful.

Charlene sent me two new books, and I have my *People Magazine*. It's gonna be a big night tonight!

There is a guy "Mo" who is going to pick up my Lincoln and sell it for me at auction. He has been doing it for years out of Springfield, Massachusetts. He is doing eight years for kicking back odometers. I think he is going to offer me a job in Vermont. It is good money from the start: Mel's Circle Auto North. "Walt, go shine your head"! It's getting dull.

Well, I gotta go now. Thanks for the letter. Lock the doors and keep the maniacs on a leash

Love,
Miro

Johnny Boy,

> The river of shit flows on.
> Friday for a change a little more nothing.
> Not a god damn thing! The fucking wind won't stop blowing!
> Blow wind, blow wind. Blow my baby back home
> to me. So I sit here broken-hearted etc.

The softball season here is having difficulty getting off of the ground. Cops won't let us pick who's on the teams. The Goombas are pissed. They may not have a team. Cops are pissed because they make money off softball, and they can't find umpires. Personally, I don't give a rat's ass. I saw two to three games I did enjoy. The king and his court were here last year.

The wind is blowing so hard that we can't play tennis. But I'm handling it, barely. Manic depression has captured my soul, but the kids will be here in another week. That will be a shot in the arm. Bugs says you guys will be down again when it gets warmer.

Winter just won't quit. It is supposed to rain for two days. Flood warnings are out. I am just working out and going to work.

I just finished reading *Papa John*, about the mammas and the pappas. Talk about druggies, those people were world-class intense!

I didn't know you had an uncle in Florida. "I got an uncle in Harlem. He's like a father to me."

So hang in there son, and keep those cards and letters coming

Your friend,
Bernard Perdee

Letter number 66, FPC Allenwood to John Kravetz

Shonny,

Well, I spoke to the kids, and they will be here tomorrow. I am excited and psyched to the max. They will visit Friday for a while and come back on Saturday. I won't be able to sleep tonight! I got a haircut and everything.

The last few days have been in the sixties and seventies and the fucking wind has been blowing 40 and 50 miles per hour. It really fucks up everything. Tennis balls just fly away. This is a great place for a fucking prison, just perfect.

I guess I can stop worrying about losing my job in the pool hall. I am still working out.

Everything else is the same. I can't wait to see the kids.

That's all for now. Be cool, my brother.

Mel

Letter number 67, FPC Allenwood to Charlene Wakefield

Hi, Chuck,

Great visit. Thanks again for bringing Travis down. The day after you left, they caught a guy having sex with his girlfriend in the kid's playroom. One of the other visitors (an old woman) told a guard so now he lives over at the *low*. His girlfriend had been dropped off by friends who were visiting at another prison. The guards dropped her off on Route 15. We missed it. Then of course there were the gays.

I just got your letter and thanks for the cards. You are right. That story about what Susan (my ex) says to the kids really does bother me. She is so negative. Her life ended the day I left. Hey, Sue, that was almost ten years ago. She wants those kids to stay with her for the rest of her life. That's why she tries to keep them down. Misery loves company. There is nothing I can do about it till I get out.

Sounds like a fun trip to Nevada. Say hello to Asia and Rachel for me. I will give my barber the compliment.

Have a good trip…

G

Charlene,

Thanks for the books. *Midnight Express* is one of the most intense books I have ever read. I don't want it to end. He makes Papillon look like a pansy. Holly shit. I can really relate to doing time. It's the same anywhere.

I got a nice letter from my daughter Gracie and a lame letter from my son Travis. So, I wrote back to Travis with eight questions for him to answer. If he uses complete sentences, there should be half a page.

I finally got fired from my recreation job. Fired wasn't really the right word. They had to get down to thirty-five people, and I wasn't a *Goomba* or a *leg hanger*. So, I didn't survive the cut.

Anyway, my buddy Jim C. got me a job in the laundry. I start Monday. I should be getting about $27.00 a month by June. It beats $4.80, plus I have been getting bored with almost nothing to do. This will definitely pass some time. I find that time is really dragging by. April took forever. May is moving a little faster. I want to look up and have it be five months later. I don't want this last year to drag. I have to be at work at 6:15 a.m., and I get done at 2:00 p.m.

Tonight, was Jimmy C.'s birthday. He was forty-four years old. He bought me ice cream. I gave him this birthday card with a kitten on it. It was so sweet. Ha ha!

I finished *Midnight Express*. I start *Mafia Princess*. It is okay. A very long-winded writer this Thomas C. Renner is. I will finish the book, but Antoinette Giancana knew very little about what her dad did.

Some guy took off from here two nights ago and spent two nights in the woods. He saw a corrections office that he recognized getting gas and asked for a ride back. He gets eighteen months added on to his sentence. He will probably spend some time in the *hole*. You got to have a plan.

I got a couple of postcards from Bugs and Grace. They went to the New Orleans Jazz Festival. Sounds like a great time. I got a picture of Gary U.S. Bonds. Remember him?

The screws started fucking with Jim M. When he is outside at work, he is allowed to go to the camp store. The hacks said he tried to pay with money. We are not allowed to have money. They reported him. The guard lied. Jim. M. only has six to eight weeks left, and they like to take away good time. The longer they keep you here, the more money they make. It is sick. Jim is really pissed. I told him he was too close to the hacks. They will never be on his side. They are always cops first. I hope he doesn't get into any trouble for being a volunteer.

Why don't blind people skydive? Because it scares the shit out of their dogs! Ha ha.

Saturday night, and I am bored to tears.

That's all folks.

G

Chuck,

I am starting a letter to you before I get one. Lots of news of late.

News flash from Prison Central: big goings-on this week. The Federal Penitentiary at Lewisburg had an open house last week, and that same day, two inmates were stabbed to death. They had the place locked down at the time too.

Then Bill Clinton passed a bill that anyone arrested who has no green card cannot get bail. That way, it is easier to deport people. Well, the bill was signed, and that day, they came to all of the prison camps, took out all *illegals* and put them behind the level-two fence. We don't have fences or walls in the camps so you can just walk away. Once they catch up with you, they add eighteen months to your sentence. They were afraid that the *illegals* were going to take off. We lost sixty guys in thirty minutes. You wouldn't believe it. They were like storm troopers. They herded them all out at the four-o'clock *count* with just whatever they were wearing. They put them on a bus to the *low-security prison*. Then they put all of their belongings in plastic bags, loaded them onto trucks, and sent them to the low. It was frightening to watch. My friends J. and George from Colombia and some Italian and Dominican guys I know all got shipped. It was real storm-trooper shit. They all got stuff stolen by some of the assholes in this place. By that, I mean *cockroach* inmates. The good news is I got a single cube out of the deal. I have never had a bad roomie, but if there is anything better than a good roomie, it's no roomie. Having a single is great, and when I get to the rehab program, I will most likely have a single.

I started work in the laundry on Wednesday. I think it is going to work out just fine. I am back up to $20.00 a month, and I am supposed to become a washer in June which will give me a pay raise to $29.00 a month. I'll take it.

It was about 90 degrees today, but the wind is still blowing. They had softball games and the movie *Jumanji*. It was okay. "American President played yesterday." It was good but total bullshit.

It is so hot that everyone is running around in shorts and no shirts outside on the patios.

I am reading *Interview with a Vampire*. That Anne Rice can really spin a yarn.

Still haven't received my Urantia book. I can't wait for it to arrive. I think I will read a paper every day. That is about all I can absorb. I just got a copy of *Be Here Now*. I love that book.

This is how much I wrote before I got your exceptionally long letter. I love details. You are always good with details. Thanks for all of the postcards. I just bought a bunch of postcard stamps. Bugs sent me a copy of *Casino* just in time. They are showing it next week. It's Memorial Day, a three-day weekend with a picnic! Burgers and dogs! You can stuff your face.

I am now reading *Be Here Now*, one of my favorite spiritual books because it shows you that they are all the same in the end. We need a book like that around here. There are so many groups of young people here looking for spiritual knowledge. They are so into trying to force their egos on each other rather than looking for similarities. I hang out sometimes with a group of guys who are Moorish Scientists. Their history is very interesting. They came from northern Africa and Asia as slaves, and they were very rebellious in this country. One of them saw me with *Be Here Now*. He said he heard that I had some interesting stuff to show him. I don't tell everyone about Urantia. People already think that I am way out there when it comes to spirituality. I can't wait for the U book.

Well, that's enough for now.

Love,
G

Hi, Carl,

Well, it's May 30th, and I am about to turn fifty years old in prison. What a depressing thought. I am also going to turn fifty-one in prison which is more depressing.

At work today I almost got into a fight with this crazy old dude. He threatened me and got in my face because I moved one of his laundry carts. He leaves in ten days, so I know he's nuts. We would have both gone to the hole, and he would be here for more than ten more days. It wouldn't have looked very good on my record what with the drug program and all. Anyway, he is gone in ten more days. That was close.

Russel's wife says that Kent has been back around Bellows Falls saying that he is going to kill Mike D. because he thinks Mike killed his son. Weird. You know Mike told me when we were locked up together that he was going to have Kent Jr. killed. When it happened, I was afraid that I would be implicated so I wrote to my lawyer and told him what I knew. We finally decided to keep quiet unless foul play was mentioned. The cops never contacted me, but if they had I would never have hesitated to tell what I knew. I don't need a murder charge. Of course, if I could get some time off, I wouldn't have hesitated to tell what I heard. Mike is no friend of mine. Anyway, I told Russel because he will tell Terry and then everyone at "Nicks" will know. If the cops contact me, what can I do? I only have a year left, but I would take some time off at Mike's expense. Russel told me that Mike wore a wire over to his, Russel's, sister's house, and that is how Russel got thirty-three months for an *eight ball.*

Two of the INS guys came back today. They made a mistake. They really were citizens. I haven't spoken to them yet.

It is finally sunny out today and in the sixties, but the wind is blowing about 40 miles an hour. This is a perfect place for a prison.

Well, take care. Thanks for the letters.

G

Dear Charlene,

It is a warm and boring Sunday afternoon in the big house. I haven't done anything but sleep and read. I did get some encouraging news though. A friend of mine was over in the drug unit, and he saw a list of names of the people who are scheduled for the October class. My name was on the list! So barring unforeseen circumstances, I should be on track. That means I am in a halfway house by next June. Also, I will be going to Boston. It is the only place in New England with aftercare for druggies.

Also, there is a guy in here from Springfield, Massachusetts. Who wants me to work for him in Vermont? He wants me to go around to new car dealerships buying the trade-ins up to be sold at auction. He says I could make up to $800 to $1000 a week. We use his money too. He gets out four months after I do. I could stay in Vermont and earn a good living. I could drive a good cat too.

So now at my next team meeting, I will ask for a furlough. I will be twenty-four months from the door. I should be able to get five days in Vermont.

Too bad Mike W. won't be joining us here at camp. He got an assault charge for dropping that garbage can on another inmate who was giving him shit overusing the phones. He now has violence on his record, so no camp for him. I can't believe he hasn't managed to work his way down to camp status. There are guys here who have done a lot worse before they got here.

God, I am really excited about getting into the October drug class. I can finally start the count down. I won't really rest until I am sleeping in C-unit. There is a committee in congress that wants to take away the year off. There has been constant tension all day long. Today a guy got into a fight. He got fired. The cops took him out, and now he works in the kitchen. My boss was ranting. I just kind of stood there.

My friend Jim can be a real asshole to work with. I let him know a couple of times today. The good thing is that five minutes later, he and I are back to being friends again. The crazy old guy that threatened me last week left for halfway house today.

So, while everyone was flipping out around me today, I just looked at my boss and laughed. Truth be told, I wouldn't be sad if he transferred me. I didn't do anything though. I think he likes me anyway. It gets really hot in there, and people go off. They are hard to read sometimes, but I am pretty good in those kinds of situations. So the river of shit flows on. Boy, it is going to be hot. We have washers and dryers the size of hot tubs.

Well, baby cakes, thanks for all of the letters.

Did I tell you about the book *Repugnant Warehouse*? It is an exposé book about this place. It tells about ways the BOP used to extend the inmates' time so the cops can get more tuition. The system here is very corrupt. It would be an interesting read, but I can't read it because it is banned here. Well, that's all for now...

Love,
G

Hey, Chuck,

Thanks for the postcards. The addition looks good. What are you going to do with all that extra room?

I was trying to call Dennis and Nancy for over a week now. They were over at Laconia, New Hampshire, for bike week. I needed to get a friend of theirs on my visiting list. They want to ride down on their Harleys. That would be great. I haven't had a visit since you, Lynn, and Travis came down. So, you can come down and stay as long as you like. I wish you could sleep over.

Kravetz's father is dying. I think he had a couple of strokes. Johnny is going to see him this weekend. I really like his dad, "Big Brad." He gave all of us our original nicknames.

Two people here just got sentence reductions cut in half for marijuana cultivation. One guy got a seventy-month reduced to thirty months. He has been down for twenty-seven months.

I am eligible for a nine-month reduction if I can get into court for resentencing, and I am thinking about it since congress is thinking about taking away the year off. It is in congress right now. That means October 1998 for me.

I am reading an erotic Western now, *The Adventures of Spur McCoy*. He gets laid in every chapter. "Nevada Hussy," "Wyoming Wildcat," "Cat House Kitten," "Rocky Mountain Vamp," "Santa Fe Floosy," the list goes on. I am going to read them all. That Spur really gets around.

I still don't have the Urantia book. Boy, I wish it would come.

Not much else to say. Keep on writing.

Love,
Spu

'Sup, kid,

It's Mel "Busta Rhymes" Miro, kickin' it with the home boys here at the FPC. We had a funk fest last week. I thought you might like a poster.

Got a letter from Mike W. today. He is twelve months from the door. So am I if things go as planned. There is always that *if.* He can't come to Allenwood Camp because he was a bad boy, too many *shots*. They won't lower his custody level. Too bad. It would be great to have him here. Jim M. leaves in a week and Russel in September. It's gonna be lonely here with just me and 800 of my closest friends.

Sorry to hear about your dad. Give him my love when you see him. I have nothing but fond memories of them all.

I am still working in the laundry. It's not bad.

Yes, I am still a vegetarian except the other day they slipped some chicken into the stir fry. You gotta watch them. I have been a vegetarian for a month now. I don't even eat sea animals.

My friend Brian finds out this month if he is coming back to jail or not.

Well, that's it for now my friend. Stay cool, my fellow Lettuce Brother.

Your pal,
Corn Bread

Well, we are the hit of the visiting room. About six people commented about us. One guy and his wife were watching people come in, and they saw this petit lady with size eleven feet, and they almost died. Charlene wore a pair of my sneakers over her sneaks. The guards never noticed but a lot of my friends did. What a scream! I won the award for the guy who had the most fun on his visit. Paulie said he wished someone like you would come and visit him. We had a good laugh, and I love my new sneaks. I washed them today, and they came out fine.

No work tomorrow, July 4th but no four-day weekend. The warden says no four-day weekend. He's got all of the hacks pissed at him. What an asshole. I don't think he will be around long. They get rotated any way.

I read the new furlough policy, and I do have a chance for one. It's a slim one, but I will try.

It is freezing here today, and these idiots have the fans on. What a bunch of jerks. I tell you it would be nice to get a few days away from here. Lately it has been unbearable.

Grace sent me a really nice letter. She got a job working for Halladay's, thirty-three hours a week. Travis is a teacher's helper again. That's good news. A little cash will help out.

Well, that's all for now. Enjoy all of the sensational news I included in this letter.

Love,
G

Johnny,

I am starting this letter early because I have this important news clip to send to you. I won't finish this letter till next week.

I am going over to A-unit in a minute to say goodbye to Jim M. He is leaving tomorrow at 8:30 a.m. for Concord, New Hampshire, to a halfway house. I can't believe it. I was here when he got here, and now, I am saying goodbye. The same thing with Russ; he leaves in September for a Boston halfway house. He got a job through someone in here working at a Pepsi trucking company. God, this prison shit is getting old.

Charlene will be here Friday and Saturday, and Dennis and Nancy will follow soon.

I am sitting tight at 200 pounds, but I feel like it is getting ready to break. My stomach is tightening up with all of the crunches, but I had to quit lifting weights because it is bringing back my bursitis. I am still walking and vegging. No sea animals, very little dairy. Mostly rice and beans. That's my Dominican roots.

Mike got a couple of shots at Butner, so he will definitely not be coming here. No camp status for him. Too bad. We should be in halfway house together. I can't wait to leave this place. They are so petty. Eleven months and counting.

Anyway, I am out of the news so keep the faith. I think I will go watch a softball game between the *Goombas* and *Los Baseball Diablos*, Latin Kings, *Los Bridgeport Torreros*!

Love,
Miro

July 4th was lame. It was cold as hell, and the tape store was closed so we watched *The Untouchables*.

Letter number 76, FPC Allenwood, to Charlene Wakefield, July 12, 1996

Hey, babe,

Well, I am disillusioned. Along with your letter, I received a notice from Whole Life products informing me that my book was refused authorization for receipt not obtained. This is the book that I went through my counselor to obtain, the one that figured would be no problem at all. I am pissed off. What is going to happen with the Urantia book? I am going to my counselor on Monday. I may have to file a religious discrimination charge on these motherfuckers. I'm gonna have to see the warden. We have Muslims, Jews, Moorish Scientists, and all kinds of Christians. This is bullshit. This place is getting to me lately.

Thank you, Angelo, for the $20. The same assholes who refused my book opened your letter and lost the money order. They never took it out, and I found it. So, I have to bring it to the business office myself. These people couldn't work any place else, glorified burger flippers.

There was a fight on HBO last night, and some of the guys got carried away. One guy who works with me punched out another guy and went to the hole. He may even get an assault charge. He could even get more time and be sent to the low (behind the fence). They also caught another guy at the White Deer motel getting some nookie. He could get more time. What price pussy! He only had three months left to go.

The laundry is a good place to work. I have been scoring underwear and socks for all my friends. My boss is crazy, but somehow we get along very well. He gave me my grade three pay raise. He still yells and jumps up and down, but he is good to his crew. If you can put up with his shit he puts up with yours. He used to work up in the maximum-security joints, and a few years ago, some inmates raped him with a broom handle. That's pretty intense.

I really hate this country. All of those things our generation was saying for twenty-five years ago are more true today. "Why be a loyal plastic robot for a world that doesn't care."

Well, this letter is becoming long.

Gotta go.
George

I love it when they call me Big Poppa. Throw yo hands in the air if you're a player!

We got a video, "A great day in Harlem!" It's about when all of the Jazz cats showed up for a group portrait. Check it out. It is very intense!

J. M. is in Concord, New Hampshire, trying to convince his future parole officer to let him work for his brother-in-law at his (J. M.'s house). Good luck with that one.

Charlene saw J. M.'s wife at the July 4th Saxtons River celebration where you were captured once again on film in the *Hairy Armpit* Parade! Also, a photo of Angelo was taken. He looks the same. I hope to be present next year.

It's raining today. It has been cold today which is good for me being that I am working in the laundry. I may go see "Twelve Monkeys" later today although it could never top "A Great Day in Harlem."

Today is hotter than hell. We have all of the fans going full blast.

My bursitis is back really bad. I may have to go to the doctor. I aggravated it by lifting weights. I was only lifting thirty-five pounds. I hope it doesn't take a year to get better like last time.

Well, take it easy, and write soon.

G

Thanks for the Georgia O'keeffe thing. I always like her. *Vamps &*
Tramps, here's Johnny, Aldous Huxley movie.

I am really bummed about my Urantia, Stillness, and Jesus
books. Yes, please send them. Lynn will send Stillness. J. M. was supposed to send a copy of the article about the *Sand Hill* bust. Eric and
Travis left just in time. Those kids are chips off the old block. What
did we expect?

Rumors are flying around here about whether or not they are
taking away our year off. It is driving me crazy. Someone else was
over at the drug unit and saw my name on the list for the next class.
I am close to the bottom. People are coming in and bumping other
people off. Supposedly if they don't cancel the year off, we are safe.
Rumors, rumors. It's driving me crazy. I try not to think about it.

My friend Jim is really happy. He just got a sentence reduction
from seventy months to forty months. That's a three-level reduction.
He has been down now for fifteen months. He may have to go to
Connecticut for resentencing. That means handcuffs and leg shack-
les via bus and plane with stays in FPC Otisville and Bridgeport,
Connecticut, jail. He was a *self-surrender*. I told him that he can't
get the full ambiance of the BOP without a trip thru Otisville. He's
funny. These investment bankers!

Today we had a new guy start work in the laundry. He was one
of Michael Milkins' lawyers. The judge hated him. He had a New
York conviction to run concurrent with fed time, and the feds left
him in Attica for eighteen months! Now that's *hard time*! He said
he doesn't know how he survived. He gave legal advice and wrote
motions for everyone, free of charge. Now he is here and thinks it is
heaven! It's still hell to me. Depression and loneliness are never far
away.

I got a check from Angelo. It never should have made it through
the mail room since we can't have money. We have nothing we can
spend it on anyway. It is supposed to go into my account. I got yelled
at for not telling my counselor that they made the mistake. I just

played dumb and thanked them for straightening it out. Just call them "Sir," and they get boners. I get the physician's assistant to give me what I want. I just call him "Doctor," and he cums in his pants! They are all legends in their own minds! This place is such a joke except it ain't funny no more.

Remember that guy from the visiting room (Eric) that time you Travis and Lynn came to visit? He just stopped by to borrow *Mob Star* (John Gotti). He did a seven-year stretch in New York State Prison. He spent three years with Gotti. This is the guy my sister thought was an *Adonis*. I should write and tell her, "Ladies love outlaws." He is a pretty friendly guy. He's tough though.

Boy, I wish I had some of my books. I am so tired of what I am reading these days. Tonight, I have a *People*.

I just gave a bunch of Urantia stuff to my friend John from Waterville, Maine. We need that Urantia book. All of those books of the month club stuff gets right in. I may have to get it sent from the publisher. I can't get mine sent because there might be a file hidden in it. Sounds like bullshit to me.

Well, that's all for now. Bedtime.

Love,
"Corn Bread"

Letter number 79

Hey, Charlene,

It was good to talk to you the other day. I have been depressed lately not knowing what was going on with the 500-hour drug program. If we make it through August without congress voting it out, we should be in the clear.

I just finished a great book on dyslexia. It explained a lot of things to me. Too bad I had to read it when I was fifty. Better late than never. I finally went to the doctor today for my shoulder. Now they say tendonitis. He gave me some anti-inflammatory drugs and told me to stay out of the weight room. It feels better already.

Today is my parent's fifty-first wedding anniversary. I called, but they must have been out.

I called my daughter Grace for fifteen minutes and ran out of time. She worked for a bunch of horticulture students, and now they want to keep her full-time. She is doing well and wants to keep it up. She graduates in June.

Go, Gracie.

Thanks, I miss you.

G

Neck Bone,

My shoulder is falling off—*tendonitis*. I haven't been to work all week. I may lose my job. Who gives a shit! Tomorrow, I make the sick call again. I can't stand the pain. I need a cortisone shot now. I can't get comfortable at night. It's hard to sleep and hard to sit. Life sucks.

Charlene sent me a Urantia book. I am going to read it cover to cover in my remaining time. The drug program is still a? Just my fucking luck. They are talking about December as a starting date.

Fort Dix prison has got to find a place for like 2,000 inmates: unsafe housing. They want to send a bunch of them to our *low* security. That means that we are going to get 160 inmates from the *low* that may or may not have *camp status*. We have some guys here now who really belong back at the *low*. So we really have got to watch our asses. At the low, they can lock you in your cell at night for protection from predators. We have no cells so these fucking maniacs will be roaming loose. Let me the fuck out of here.

Glad to hear that your dad is doing better.

I hear from Charlene all of the time just like you. I wouldn't be surprised if she shows up again soon.

I just asked my Puerto Rican neighbor if he ever heard of the Macarena. He jumped up and gave me a demonstration. "Comic relief!" He says it is like the "Lambatta," but he thinks it originated in Spain. Oh, he's excited now. He's on the good foot! Switched to the other leg! Chris Matos, the Puerto Rican tailor and Macarena expert.

Well, dude keep the faith. Who loves ya, brother? Remember, the *monkey* doesn't do anything but signify. Give me the *dog* every time!

Love,
Corn Bread/Red Dog Philly Freeze/Cooka Ratcha

Johnny,

Just saw HBO's *Gotti*. Very interesting watching it here with a room full of Goombas!

My tendonitis is killing me. These motherfuckers are making me wait a month to see a doctor. I have eleven more days to wait. I have been out of work for a week and a half now. I am in constant pain. That cortisone shot would stop the pain in a matter of minutes. Never get sick in prison. They don't give a shit. They are used to being sued. They just pay.

I'm going to go see *Dusk Till Dawn* today. Quentin Tarantino's vampire movie. It should be good.

The good news is that we have a teacher for the October drug class, so I should be going over next month. I pray every day that if congress doesn't do away with the year off, I am out in June. Pray, pray, pray.

Charlene sent me a Urantia book. I am reading it cover to cover. It is mind-expanding. Every day I read a paper or two. That's all the brain-stretching I can handle at one time

In *Dusk Till Dawn*, Cheech says, "Welcome to pussy heaven! We got all kinds of pussy. Buy one pussy, get one pussy for one cent. If you can find cheaper pussy any place else, *fuck it*!"

Love,
Corn Bread

Johnny Boy,

Thanks for the $3.00, but you can't send me cash. I could go to the hole for having bills in my possession. Now they have to do a pile of paperwork. Anyway, it's the thought that counts. Fuck them.

The Yankees won last night. I am rooting for them along with the rest of the New York City posse.

Gloria Estefan is doing a concert on HBO next weekend. I want Bugs to tape it, but I hope he will be here for a visit. So you should be here too. I can't wait. It's Bugs and Grace's 25th anniversary. *Wow*.

The weather has been beautiful. I'm still in my bed all day. I have a guy in here who is a physical therapy *inmate*, and he is stretching my arm out. It is a little better. I spend my day reading the Urantia book. I would never have this much time in the real world.

I just read *The Secret Life of Jesus Christ*. It was very interesting. Actually, I read two or three books at a time. It's like changing channels. I am reading the autobiography of Anthony Quinn. He was a real womanizer.

Also I am taking a bunch of classes, tarot cards and natural preventive medicine, taught by some doctor who was on the lecture circuit. Now he is on this circuit.

I can't wait to get back to work though. I got too much time on my hands. It slows things down.

Our resident Chinese guy says he doesn't eat no rice in jail, only noodles. "That's why I lose 30 pounds." Ah so!

I just got called back to my counselor's office. The whole system has broken down all because you sent me three dollars. They don't know what the fuck to do! It's really comical. They may make me send it back to you. Do you believe it?

Well, dude, get your ass down here.

Love and kisses,
Mel "Red Chicken" Miro

Letter number 83 to Charlene Wakefield from FPC Allenwood, August 29, 1996

Hey, babe,

I saw the orthopedic doctor today. No shot, no pills, just exercise. He also gave me another month off from work. At first, I was very pissed off, but I went and did the exercise, and it turns out that it works much better than the pills that upset my stomach. I haven't had to take any Tylenol all day. I took fifty a day for a while. Tomorrow I have to make *sick* call to renew my idle. I'm gonna just keep on doing the exercises. It still hurts.

Tonight I also got a letter from my sister Lynn. She sent me a book about angels. She just got back from Antigua. She loved it and wants to move there to teach. I always felt that way whenever I got back from the islands.

Your letter was excellent, jam-packed with information. It is nice to find other Urantia folks close by. I've got John Z. from Waterville, Maine, all excited about the U book. He is reading the stuff that you sent me right now. I only had it in my hands for about ten minutes. When my son Nebadon was a toddler, Susan and I took him to the Urantia Foundation in Chicago. We were very new to the book and just decided to drop in to check it out. We met a man named John. He was about forty years. He seemed puzzled by us, trying to see just how into it we were. We were into it enough to name our son Nebadon. According to the Urantia book, we live in the universe of Nebadon. Our creator son is Christ Michael of Nebadon. We got a tour of the place but were not allowed upstairs where some people like Helaine lived. She was one of the original Urantia people. We also saw a woman named Christy.

By the way, don't send me any more books. I have to get rid of some stuff before I move to the drug treatment unit.

The other day they caught one of the gay guys wearing a G-string under his pants. They wrote him up for that. We have been taking a lot of shit lately. We had a riot alert three days ago.

Our two grievance reps got into a beef with the inmate relations people and were both sent to the hole. So the next day no one went to lunch. Out of 800 people, twenty people ate. So, the new warden locked the whole place down and interviewed all of us one by one asking us all if we were going to eat supper. Guys signed statements saying they were not eating supper. Everyone who signed is gone and not just to the hole. They can never come back. I slept through the whole thing. My shoulder was killing me... This whole thing started when the warden took away a halfway house for people with sentences less than eighteen months. Has nothing to do with me. I get a six-month halfway house for doing the 500-hour drug program. I sure as hell ain't going to jeopardize that for some *skid bidders*.

Well, by the time you get this letter, you may or may not have come to visit. I hope you did.

Love,
G

Charlene,

Well, Dennis and Nancy were here Friday and Saturday for a visit. I have to go and check my visitor list. You are not on it, at least not yet. Here is another form in case the other one got lost. We had a nice visit. It was good to see them.

It got very cold here today. We had to break out the winter coats. The wind blows steady, here and sometimes it is unbearable. Let winter come so it can be over, and I can come home. This place is pretty. Kravetz says it is a poor imitation of Vermont.

I just got a nice letter from Bugs and Grace. Bugs sent me some pictures of Neb. One of them was taken on the day of his birth. They were present for his home birth. Kravetz sent me a picture of him Owl and Bugs.

Today is my day off and the movie they are showing is *Pulp Fiction*. I have been waiting to see this one for a while. The only thing that sucks is the BOP gets its movies from the airlines who heavily censor them so as not to offend anyone viewing on the flights. I guess they don't want to shock any of us convicts, ha ha! After the flick, I will walk my four miles and play a little tennis. I played all day yesterday. That's about as good as it gets.

There is a new guy named Billy here from Maine. He just got seventy months for growing pot. That's a pretty stiff sentence. His defense was that he was nuts, and for the past twenty-eight years, he has been smoking it in place of his medication which he is now back on. He used to work in food service with me, but it was too stressful so his shrink put him on grounds keeping which means he walks around all day with a stick with a nail in the end picking up litter. When the Canadian geese arrive to have their chicks, it means that you get to scoop up goose shit for six months. The shrink wants Billy close by. Anyway Grounds and Horticulture are getting a greenhouse, and we all thought how nice it would be to work there. Billy told his boss that he used to grow pot, and he told his boss that I did too, and I that I also wanted a job. His boss wrote a note to my boss asking for me. "This inmate has invaluable knowledge." My boss won't let me go. Too bad, I am tired of the kitchen.

I am going to try for a soft-shoe permit. You can't work in the kitchen without steel-toe shoes. They really do hurt my feet.

Well, that's all of the excitement for now. I am going to be easily pleased when I get out of here. Say hi to everyone for me.

George

Neck Bone,

So, you got a hippie roomie young enough to be your daughter getting loaded with her friends in your living room. Does she know Wally the *rainbow-gathering* hippie friend of Charlene?

Charlene came to visit me this weekend. We got into trouble for being too affectionate in the visiting room. Next time they will bust me.

Just came from a salesmanship class. My friend Tom teaches it. Also, a history class, a tarot class, and sports medicine class. That should give you an idea of how bored I am.

Charlene and I had our pictures taken together, and I got them back today. They came out very well. I am sending her one today.

I have been on *idyl* now for six weeks. All I do is read and sleep. I finally got a Urantia book in, so I read one paper that blows the top of my head right off. I can't digest much more than that at once.

My arm is much better, but it still hurts. I got a guy who stretches it out for me twice a day. I started riding the exercise bike forty minutes a day. I don't want to gain any weight. Other than that, things have been uneventful. I just want to get this shit over with and get the fuck out of here.

Stay cool.

Miro

Letter number 86, FPC Allenwood, September 18, 1996, to Charlene Wakefield

Chuck,

Fact: The stock market always goes up on the 13th of Friday. They keep it that way. People are superstitious. Your broker bought and sold so that he can get paid. Anyway, as long as you get paid.

J. M. is in Texas turning states evidence on his friends down south. J. M. could be looking at a serious time this time (two-time looser). Thanks for the postcards. I need plenty so I could send them to Bugs. He can't face his mailman!

I spoke to my kids. Travis will be a freshman. They don't say much on the phone.

By the way, Bugs and Owl will be here on the 28th. Hop in the car.

I am still on idyl. I'm spending my days sleeping and reading. Still stretching my arm. It's a little better. Two more weeks till I get to see the doctor again.

Bugs and Grace celebrated their 25th wedding anniversary.

Did you get a chance to get me a good version of *Saturn Return?*

I am reading *The Unknown Life of Jesus*. Not very interesting. I think I will stick to the Urantia book. Thanks for the Urantia stuff. I ran into another guy in here who is into the U book. He says his brother has read it seven times. Now his seventeen-year-old son is reading it. Another Muslim friend wants to check it out. Some of the Moorish Scientists are interested. If I can present things properly, no one will think I am putting down their religion.

Well, that's all for now.

Love,
G

Johnny,

Bugs and Owl couldn't make it. Caroline's folks were coming into town. Every week that they don't come to visit, I send them another embarrassing postcard. His mailman thinks he's a pervert! Wait till I get through with him! The only trouble is I am having trouble figuring out the order of intensity myself. Charlene sent me one tonight that may have scorched its way to number one. It may be against the law to mail. Anyway, he gets another one tonight.

By the way, I finally got the $3.00 you sent into my account.

The feds took J. M. out of the halfway house in Concord and shipped him to Austin, Texas. Probably his partner in Texas was popped last Christmas so somehow they found a connection between those two. They have been doing shit for the past thirty years. Boy, what a kick in the nuts that must be for J. M. He could go away for *all day* behind this case. Charlene saw Laima, and she said SST said that J. M. ratted out B. I don't think that is true. He was here with me when B got popped. It's probably the other way around. Else, why did they come up here for J. M.? I will keep you posted.

Yeah, the Urantia book people have come a long way since we first got into it in the seventies. I subscribe to a couple of new letters. I am reading the U book again, and it is stretching my mind. I love this book. It goes beyond religion. If you ever want to check it out, we placed one in the Bellows Falls library in Nebadon's name. Any spiritual person would be interested in this book. It answers questions I never thought to ask. The authors are celestial personalities in service to the father in heaven.

The planet of Urantia is in the Universe of Nebadon. There are 600 planets in this universe. Nebadon is entrusted to a paradise son of God known as Michael. This is his universe, and he is in charge of the spiritual evolution of all of his father's mortal beings. You and I are two of these beings. Anyway, Michael incarnated on this planet 2,000 years ago in the personality of Jesus of Nazareth to try and give us a clue. It's a book you can read for the rest of your life. All questions are answered, and the history is an eyewitness account because the authors (personalities) were there. It's up close and personal.

So now you have another chance to hop in the car and come visit.

Love,
Mel

Hey, Charlene,

Russel is leaving tomorrow. His wife Teri is already at the White Dear Motel waiting for him. I'm glad he is out, but I will miss him. Now if I could only get over to that drug unit for the next class, I will walk out of here in August.

Celestine Prophecy is one of the best books I have ever read. I can't put it down.

My arm is finally getting better. I think I will finally be seeing the doctor tomorrow morning. Whether or not he gives me a cortisone shot is another story. I can't stay on idyl anymore. I am bored stiff.

I found another Urantia book reader in here, and I turned another guy on to it. We have spiritual discussions in the unit during the day. I also found a couple of Edgar Casey freaks. We are *new-age commandos*!

The head of the drug program told one of the guys he would hire two new counselors if he could find them.

Bob came up to me and told me that Brian lost his appeal. That is no surprise. Bob's lawyer has been watching the case.

Well, the orthopedic surgeon came last Thursday, and they wouldn't let me see him. I didn't push it. I just went off idyl and back to the laundry sorting socks and underwear. I brought up about ten pairs of socks and some T-shirts and gave them away. I lost my washing job, but that's okay. I had to go back to work. What I really needed to do was use my arm so that's what I am doing.

Been eating scones hey! I haven't had one of them since my poor old Irish grandmother made me some with a cup of tea. That was thirty years ago.

Well, love thanks for the letter. Write back soon.

Love,
G

Johnny,

"Stop what you're doin', 'cause I'm about to ruin, the image and the style that you're used to."

Just came back from seeing *Twister*. It was better than I expected. Hellen Hunt was very good. I want her!

Bugs and Owl canceled their visit till the weekend of October 26th. So hop in the car.

Charlene sent me a clipping of some woman in Westminster, Vermont, who was busted with fifty-five pot plants. She got a ticket. Good thing the DEA wasn't involved. She would be on her way to FCI Danbury (woman's prison) for a sixty-month stretch. This country is out of control. Stay in Vermont, the land of the free.

The weather here has been beautiful. We just had a three-day weekend. They slow things down. I would rather work.

I started exercising again. The arm is much better. Time to tighten up. I haven't done a crunch in two months.

I am taking a tarot card class. October 5th is my mom's birthday. I called her.

I just got back from my tarot reading. It was my second one. It was okay. My teacher did readings in Vegas for $20.00 for a ten-minute reading. Gamblers are very superstitious.

I just finished the first section of the Urantia book, *The Super Universe*. It was too intense. I only understood about 30 percent. Next is the *Local Universe*. That should be more comprehendible. I will keep you posted.

Gotta go teach my class.

Love,
Zoot Horn Rollo

Hey, babe,

I just Xeroxed a paper from Urantia on *Celestial Musicians*. I am going to send it to Kravetz. It will blow him away! I take my Urantia book to work now every day and read for about two hours. I am knocking it out and getting into it more and more. My friend John Z. from Waterville, Maine, got a letter from his grandma. She bought a U book also. She is hooked. We are having fun!

I did a tarot reading tonight for my son, Travis. It came out pretty good. I am gonna send it to him for his birthday, November 6th. He will be sixteen years. I feel so bad about missing it. Next week I will do one for Gracie.

Kravetz saw Slappy drive by with Travis, Grace, Fern, and April in his '54 Chevy. That must have been a sight!

Tomorrow I finally get to see the orthopedic surgeon, big deal. I have been working for a month. My arm is a lot better, but I still have a long way to go. Maybe I will finally get that cortisone shot.

Jimmy C. is going out on a writ to Connecticut on Nov 1st. He is a washer so I will be taking his place. I kind of like doing other stuff mostly because I have time to read the U book.

That's interesting about being eligible for Irish citizenship. I am only a second-generation American. The best part is Ireland has no extradition treaty with the US. I gotta stop thinking that way!

There was just a new law passed—no more naked lady magazines allowed in federal prison. They start enforcing it on January 1, 1997. *Playboy* and *Penthouse* are suing the feds. It is freedom of the press. The magazines stand to lose $100,000,000 a year. It should be a really interesting battle. I wonder what they will do about the *Easy Rider* mag!

Well, that's all for now. Say hi to everyone.

Love,
G

Letter number 91 to John Kravetz, FPC Allenwood, October 27, 1997

Johnny,

Well, Bugs and Owl came to visit, and a pleasant time was had by all. And then the Yankees won. Cool. They tore this place apart. Half of the people here are from the Bronx. Everyone was happy. Old Yankee fans couldn't believe it. There were tears in people's eyes! The celebration went on till dawn.

I got a letter from Slappy with pictures of his '54 Chevy and one of Gracie and him and pictures of Curtis' Pavilion of Swine. Bugs said he was up there about a month ago to pick up some sauce.

I just went down to the weight pile to see if my shoulder was strong enough for me to hang in my slings to do leg raises. They are not. I will try again in a month or two. I am back on the stair monster and walking.

I am taking the Urantia book to work every day. I get about two hours of reading in a day. I ran across a paper last week that you might find interesting. *Celestial Musicians*, check it out. This book is better than acid man! Gad the colors!

Well, dude it is about time for lunch. I'm gonna get me some flap jacks then go see a movie.

Love,
MM

Hi, Charlene,

Got a Halloween card from my son Travis and my daughter Grace with pictures. They were great. So I called the house and talked to them. Gracie is having trouble with high school credits. She may not graduate unless she makes up some Shakespeare course. She was pretty bummed out. I talked to her for a half-hour. I called just in time. She gets her driver's license on Thursday. Thanks for going over there and taking pictures.

Thanks for the books. They look good, just in time. I read 500 pages of the Urantia book.

Great visit with Owl and Bugs. Kravetz couldn't make it. We had a great time. I sent Sharon one of your postcards. I am having so much fun with those cards. Man, they are intense!

I am friends with the guy who takes care of the greeting cards, and he gave me four or five birthday cards for Travis. His birthday is coming up on November 6th. I really wish I could be around for that.

My friend Jimmy C is going out on a rit to Connecticut for a sentence reduction. He will get at least fifteen months off. He could get as much as thirty months off. Anyway I am doing his job in the laundry. It's not bad but less time to read the U book. I got up to the *Lucifer Rebellion* today, and it made a lot more sense. There is lots of cool stuff about how this planet would be if our evolution had not been interrupted. I am so glad that I have this book. It makes all the difference in the world to me.

I just got back from class and found letters from you and Marilyn, Brian's friend. Brian is back in jail. She has some questions about getting Brian's sentence reduced. My friend John wrote a whole motion for another guy here, and the guy is home now. I went immediately over to him, and he is rounding up his stuff to send to Brian. That ten-year mandatory minimum is gonna be a tough one. I hope they send him here. He was a flight risk, so he will probably go to the low security up the road.

I finally waded through the really intense part of the U book. I made it to *The History of Urantia*, and it is clear sailing from here on in. I understand everything. I am reading from ninety billion years to fifty billion. There are still no life carriers although the planet is registered and named Urantia. Oceans and mountains have appeared.

The last section on the Local Universe spoke of what Urantia would be like if the Lucifer rebellion had not occurred. Then the last three papers had to do with the higher ideals of science, philosophy, and art.

Thanks for all of the new cards. They are always enjoyed.

Love and kisses,
G

Johnny Boy,

I just sent Angelo a visiting form. He is headed to marathon Texas to open a pizza joint, and he wants to stop by on the way. That will be cool.

Owl, Bugs, and I had a good visit. The only thing missing was you, you dirty heuer! Next time I see you, I'm gonna kick your ass! I'm gonna get you in a Russian chain fight and crush you between my massive thighs! "Destroy, destroy!" Take it easy, Nicky. He didn't mean it!

My daughter Gracie's birthday is March 3rd. Charlene is taking pictures for the yearbook. There is a guy here who paints portraits. I am going to have him do one of Gracie's. It will make a nice gift.

I got a card from Mike W. He'll be out in seven and a half months. He is involved with Debbie Z. I think they will be getting married when he gets out and are moving to Florida. We are supposed to be getting out at the same time, but I haven't even started the drug program yet. So, you won't be seeing me for a while.

My OEX student is here, so I will write more later. His name is Jermaine. He made good money tonight. The young man went out and made a name for himself, been on every record-breaking show at the Regal Theatre for the past five years.

"Let's everybody shout and shimmy!" Give the drummer some. Who wants to die for art? I gave you a hook. What more do you want? Remember when you were born cheap you die cheap! Merry Christmas, you bunch of fucking losers! Tangents, tangents, gad the colors! I can see clearly now... It's all a pattern.

My laundry customer just came by. He is a Vietnamese guy... rich motherfucker. He pays me $3.00 a week to wash his clothes with mine. He gets same-day service, and I get some cash. I don't mind paying cash for gash as long as it's class! Oh, baby, I'm hot tonight!

Be cool, my brother. I will be thinking of you.

Love,
Bernard Purdee

Letter number 94 to Charlene Wakefield, November 6, 1996, FPC Allenwood, Montgomery, Pennsylvania

Hey, hey,

I just called the house to wish my son, Travis, a happy birthday, but he was downtown. I asked my wife Sue if he would be home tonight, and she didn't know. God, she pisses me off. The kid never goes to school. I feel so helpless. I wrote him a letter about that shit. He is going down the tubes, and there is nothing I can do about it.

Fuck.

My friend Jim went out on a writ and had twenty-five months taken off his sentence. He should be getting out around the same time as me.

Thanks for the pictures of the kids. Grace and Travis sent me some pictures that you or Sue took them. She cut off Gracie's head, but still, I love getting pictures of my kids. Travis always looks so sad. It makes me feel the same.

Good luck with your angel postcards. I have gotten at least five catalogs. Angels are in it seems.

Thanksgiving is just around the corner then December 1st will be two years for me here.

Still no drug program. They say that I missed the December class. It could be a rumor, but I don't think so. Congress didn't get rid of the year off, but it ain't gonna do me much good if they keep bouncing me out of the classes. I already lost a potential six months off. I am getting very discouraged. I hate these people.

Prison is essentially a shortage of space made up for by a surplus of time. To an inmate both are palpable.

Well, babe, I am out of things to say so I guess I will say good-bye for now.

Love,
G

Johnny Boy,

Got a bad cold this week. It's the first one in years. It comes from sleeping in a room with sixty other guys. I went to the movies last night and saw *West Side Story*—when you're a jet, you're a jet all the way! I hope you enjoy the Rita Marley story. I got a card from Tavis today. He just turned sixteen.

I made it halfway through the Urantia book today, page 923. It gets more and more intense all the time. It helps to make my time go by faster. My mind is stretching! Gad the colors! You gotta read this book before you die. I know you read some when we were at the yellow house.

I am still working in the laundry. I am on *skid mark patrol!* They don't say Haines unless I say they say Haines, motherfucker."

I'll kick your ass!

Tomorrow is *The Nutty Professor*, and Sunday is *Mission Impossible*. We are also having a violin concert. I will check that out for sure.

Two inmates were killed last week in a knife fight over at Lewisburg. That's where Tuba is.

I started taking some psychology courses with our resident headshrinker, the *Bradshaw tapes*. Very interesting. It's in preparation for the drug program.

Well, I gotta go now.
Peace, love, and soul.

Your pal,
Don Cornelius

Hey, babe,

Thanks for the cards. They are always a hit.

Mark Tapper, hey. I was thinking about him the other day. I wonder what he wants. He gets no money.

I am heartbroken again about the drug program, but there is nothing I can do. Some guy went over there the other day all pissed off for not getting in the next class. He is now in the hole! Don't forget this is still a prison, and we are not free men. So here I sit. The next chance is in February which will give me four months off. These people are truly evil. They don't care. No one does. How can a convicted drug offender hope to find sympathy from the general public? At fifteen months from the door, if I get in, I will only get six-month halfway house. If I don't do the program, I will get five-month halfway house. The aftercare treatment is intense with *X* amount of NA meetings a day or week—drug counseling, piss tests, and no time off. That's what I have to think about. It's them against us. When they look at us, they see a walking $160.00 a day in their budget. It behooves them to keep us as long as they can. So they bring in new guys with shorter outdates and put them in ahead of us. They get paid twice, $40.000, for everyone they graduate from the 500-hour class. They are just protecting their own jobs at the expense of our freedom and our families. That's America at work.

I got another guy interested in the U book. He keeps trying to borrow it, but the book is already working overtime with John and me reading away. He needs to order his own. I am almost finished with the *Life of Jesus*.

I have to go photocopy the part about where you go after you die. I need to send it to my mom. Her sister is dying of cancer. The part about being able to see your loved ones for ten days will be very comforting to her.

Well, I gotta go now. Write soon.

G

Kravetz,

Hey, dude… Still chillin' like a villain with the rest of my homies. Thanks for the fabulous Moolah. I love her!

Well, turkey day is upon us once more; my second one in this place, December 1. I am here two years and down thirty-two months. I missed the drug program again. These pig-poking, goat-ropin', finger-fuckin', dick-suckin' sons of dirty heuers are inserting it squarely up my poop shoot. It's the royal rheem job! Now I can't get any more than five months off my sentence. Seg off.

I read all the Urantia books with the exception of _The Life and Teachings of Jesus Christ_. I am about fifty pages into that right now. I am up to his twelve year. His birthday is on August 21st by the way. This part of the book is really great. Reading this book is one positive thing about being here. I never would have taken the time to read it on the outside.

I'm going to send all the wrestling letters you sent me to the _Bugatorium_ for safekeeping. Classic stuff!

It's fucking freezing here today, snowy, windy, freezing, sucky… very depressing. I ate a pint of frozen yogurt, a no-no for the diet. Look out Thursday for the Thanksgiving feast. Have to double up on those stair master sessions. I can't seem to lose any pounds, but I am not gaining. Thank God.

Anyway, that's the story, Jerry. I gotta go read some more of the Urantia book.

Be cool, my brother. Peace, power, and soul.

Love,
Ziggy Stardust

Johnny Boy,

We had a Thanksgiving here that would scare ya. We are still eating turkey. It was great and needed by us all…a little holiday cheer.

I just came back from a Christmas concert in the chapel. It was a bell choir, at the Methodist Church. There were young girls playing the bells and singing Christmas carols for us jailbirds.

It snowed here, but it's gone. Our retarded warden decided to cut down chow our chow lines from two to one. It took twice as long to feed us. Everyone was pissed especially the food service staff.

They can't stand the warden, and the warden hates it here. He needs to go back to Otisville where he came from.

I am on page 1,389 in the Urantia book. I just read about the apostles. They are getting ready to go out preaching. This is the best book I have ever read in my life. I only have about 500 pages left to go, and I don't know what I will do when I am finished. I will probably start over and read it slowly just a little bit a day. I am glad I finally got to read it. I have known about it for twenty-five years.

We have a lot of religious activities around this place. We have every religion. We had a gospel group in here last year. I hope they return. The bells were excellent. The chaplain is strange. We think he is gay, but that doesn't make him a bad guy.

I didn't make the drug class again. I can't get any more than four months off my sentence. What happened to that year off?

So, keep the faith, and I will try to keep mine. Till then, I'm hangin' in like Gunga Din!

Love,
Mel

Good news! They called me over to C-unit today and wanted to know if I was still interested in taking the 500-hour drug class. Of course, I said yes, so I will be moving over to C-1 on December 30th for the class that starts at the beginning of February. If that holds true, I will be out of here next November with six months halfway house and four months off of my sentence. It is better than nothing, baby! I feel like I have taken a step forward anyway. I have a friend names George Bushey who is a clerk over there. We keep on answering each other's pages.

He is giving me a single cube in C-1. That's the high-rent district, the quietest section over there. Anyway, that's the good news.

I got a letter from Brian B. today thanking me for the info I sent him. I am going to try and get him some info on more than 1,000 plants. He should do fine.

It's the weekend, and I started another OEX student. I don't know what I will do with him once I move to C-unit in sixteen days. I won't be allowed over here anymore. If they catch me, I will get a *shot*, and one *shot* will get me thrown out of the class. I'm going to have to meet him in the library.

It's going to be a pain, but he really seems eager. He just showed up, so I am going to close for now.

People are complimenting you on those angel postcards.

There is a guy (inmate) running around here saying that it is a sure thing that after the inauguration, Clinton will be signing that will double the *good time*. That could double the good time. That could subtract eight and a half months off my sentence. That would be most excellent!

I have been hanging out with Bobby Angona. He was one of Michael Milken's lawyers. Giant corporate deals, mob ties: Atlantic City and Vegas intrigue. The guy is funny. He wants to come visit Vermont.

Well, this letter was longer than I expected. Keep in touch.

Love,

G

Johnny Boy,

Que passa, amigo? I'm still chillin'. I talked to my mother tonight. Her sister died. She was eighty-two years. It was time. Mom is doing okay.

We had an intense Thanksgiving here. There was plenty of grub to go around. I gained two pounds. Then I lost it again.

Yeah, the drug program really rheemed me this time. I'm still squealing from the feelin', oinking from the boinkin', reekin' from the freekin'. Pencil neck geeks. The river of shit flows on. Not a god-damn thing.

Christmas time in the joint! I suppose it could be worse than other places, but I just try not to think about it. It's here before you know it and gone just as fast.

I got a Christmas card from Bugs and Grace today. I sent out cards yesterday and will send out more tomorrow. Then it's goodbye '96 and hello 1997 and hopefully goodbye to these pricks.

I also got a letter from my friend Brian B. who was captured by *Unsolved Mysteries.* His girl lives in Cornish, New Hampshire. I am expecting him back here along with Jim M. who will plead guilty to conspiracy in Texas with Birdy and a cast of thousands in six states. He expects to get three more years. I won't be alone much longer.

So have a pleasant holiday. And remember Jesus's birthday is August 21st. No big deal. The 25th is fine.

Peace on ya.

Love,
Jailhouse Mel

El Monk,

Good news, I am in the February drug class! I move over to C-unit on December 30. I feel like some progress is being made. This puts me in a halfway house next November. The light at the end of the tunnel.

So you made it to the Big Apple. Cool. I love it. I would still like to live there for a while. It is still the greatest city in the world. I watch Seinfeld every day and it makes me feel like I am there. Also, half of the people in here are from there.

Gotta go. I just wanted to tell you the good news.

Miro

Happy Holidays, dude. We work a half-day tomorrow and then we get presents from the Bureau of Prisons, usually toiletries. Then we are off till the day after Christmas. They will have movies and music playing for us all day. It's just another day if I have to be here. I don't care how much I work if I have to be here.

I am moving over to the drug unit on December 30th, but the class doesn't start till February. They drag their feet. Everyday extra we are here is one more day they get paid. This will be my last Christmas in the joint if, in fact, we stay on schedule. and people stop coming in with *door* dated closer than mine. I can still be bumped. I have twenty pages left in the Urantia book

Fingers are crossed.

Love,
Miro

Christmas Eve:

Got your letter today thanks. I finished the Urantia book yesterday. Wow! That was the best book I ever read. I want to read it again at some point.

Thanks for the letter and stuff from Mike. He is really getting out great. I should be out around November if things go on schedule. People have been writing their congressmen about how this place has been dragging its feet. One guy is personal friends with Senator Patrick Lahey. Maybe we can speed things up a bit. I move over on December 30. Class doesn't start till February. That doesn't make sense to me. I can't wait till I am in the building. and it's a lock for me.

Write C-1 on my letters after December 1st.

I finally spoke to Travis and Grace tonight, Christmas Eve.

Christmas Day:

Merry Christmas

I am glad I got hold of the kids last night. The line for the phones is around the block.

Ever read about Joseph Waldholtz? His wife was a congresswoman from Utah. He stole a couple of million in campaign funds. She divorced him, said she knew nothing about it, the usual drill. Anyway, he is here. I had dinner with him last night. He says Bill Clinton has hot and cold running hookers in and out of the White House day and night. It's not surprising to me. He also says Hillary is a bigger bitch than Nancy Reagan. Here's a tidbit for you. "I'm surrounded." This guy is a real piece of work.

I am also hanging around with Bob Angona. He is a real education. He was one of Michael Milken's lawyers. He wants to give a course on corporate leveraged buyouts with his big-time banker buddies, but the education department thinks it's a subversive activity. These people are amazing. I'm swimming around in a corporate shark tank with the wiz kids. I tell you it's a trip.

Well, I just had my Christmas Dinner. We had Cornish game hens and lots of pastry. It was good. Then we saw *Cable Guy*. It was disappointing. I got lots of money from friends. I sent them all to thank you cards. I also got another letter from Brian and his girl Marilyn. I hope he does okay. I'd hate to see him get that ten-year mandatory minimum. Then he would have four years left to do. Joe Waldholtz, the congresswoman's husband, says there is a bill in congress now to double the good time. He doesn't think it will pass because it is part of the new crack bill. They hate black crack dealers. If it did pass and was retroactive, I could subtract eight months and ten days from my sentence, and Brian could subtract sixteen months if he gets ten years. If that happens, it will be in April, and I would be done. They would have to send me straight home. I'll take it.

Well, that's all the news as of this printing.

Love,
Me
Happy Holidays!

I finally moved over to C-unit today, and they told me that I had letters over there by mistake because I am now living in the _crack house_, and there was a letter from y'all. Well shit fire and save the matches.

I also got a letter—Christmas card from Lou Corbett. He saw Charlene at Christmas and got my address. He is going to Burma in February.

I would love to travel the world like he does. I may do it too.

Dallas Cowboys are on their way in. I guess it's the Pats and Packers now. I like the Jaguars—Jaguars, yes the Jaguars. Curiously refreshing! Fantastic view of the harbor, boats, and all that! "Yes splendid Holmes." Elementary, my dear Watson. Seg off, what. Alright, enough of this bullshit. You really think I got no class. I need a shirt I can wear four or five days in a row where you can't notice the dirt. They don't go to the bathroom here. "Take it easy, Nicky. He didn't mean it."

I'm sitting here thinking just how sharp I am. I'm the under-assistant West-Coast promo man. Actually, I'm thinking where the fuck are those hacks who are late with the count. I'm hungry, and I want to go see _Joe's Apartment_, dancing cockroaches. "_La cucaracha, la cucaracha,_" _yo no puedo caminar la la la_! Hey Leroy, your mama she calling you, man. I'm a no-talk, so good! You need a bullet. Gad the colors! Suzzy crème cheese oh baby now what got into ya! Brown shoes don't make it. Quit school. Why fake it?

You should have been to the last party. We didn't get home till four in the morning. I was blind for three days!

The FBI showed up here yesterday. One inmate conned a couple of others out of $100,000 bucks. He is fucked. They won't even have a trial, just tack on another ten years. Don't fuck with the feds. It's their bat and their ball, and this ain't our field. And the shoes of the fisherman ain't no jive-ass sandals. Somebody stop me! I'm on a roll. Roll another one just like the other one.

I got a lot of great new stuff from the Urantia people.

See ya dude. Keep those cards and letters coming.

Love and kisses,
Corn Bread

Letter number 105, FPC Allenwood, January 3, 1997, to Charlene Wakefield

Hi, Chuck,

This is my first letter to you from C-unit (the crack house). I moved over two days ago.

At least now I can know a little bit better when this nightmare will end. The first weekend in December '97. I should be out of here. That's eleven months away. It's very nice over here, quiet all the time and not very crowded. My friend George who I met twenty-five months ago is now the unit clerk, and he got me a single cube. Thanks, George.

I just finished *Exit to Eden* yesterday. I loved it. I'm now starting *Story of O* and reading *Ishmael* at the same time. Now that I have finished the Urantia book, I am back up to speed. I also have some reading to do for my technical analysis class.

My Urantia calendar ended so enclosed please find the final page. I wrote them a letter with my favorite quote: "As long as we teach the child to pray 'Our father who art in heaven,' a tremendous responsibility rests upon all earthly fathers to live and order their homes so that the word Father becomes worthily enshrined in the minds and hearts of all growing children." I love that quote. I want to print up some and give them to all the young guys here in parenting class.

On January 1st, we have to get rid of all our colored T-shirts and other extra clothes, lots of new rules. I can only have twenty-five photos. I have a lot more than that. I am afraid of losing my Nebadon pics. I am going to hide them when they shake us down. I must have had twenty pairs of socks. You can only have five. I will replace them once they shake us down. That's one of the benefits of working in the laundry.

I was offered the warden's orderly job, but I turned it down. I can't be too close to that piece of shit. I will stay in the laundry.

My boss went crazy today. Maybe I should have gone to that warden's job. No, things will blow over.

Just got your letter today (January 2). Sounds like Christmas was pretty stressful. I just put it out of my mind. I called the kids to say MC and went to bed. On New Year's Eve I was asleep at ten. This place was so quiet I didn't wake up till 7 a.m. We had T-bone steaks, and I had to break them apart so nobody could make a shiv! Do you believe that?

I think you are right about giving *Mort* information to W. C. I am not telling him anything else.

Well, dear, that's all for this week.

Love and kisses,
Me

Hi, Chuck,

Well, I'm all settled down in C-unit. It's too quiet. I keep on over-sleeping. We had a wake-up club over in B-unit. I will get used to it. I like it here. They're only about twenty-five guys in my unit, and most of us have single cubes. If only I could wake up for work.

There is going to be a big meeting here soon. It will be like a town meeting to let them know what is going on with this place. It takes nine months to do a class when we only go to class seven hours a week. How they delay classes, eliminate teachers, and whole classes. How they drag their feet in any way they can to delay everyone's release date. They misrepresent the number of people in the unit. Lots of guys over here have graduated, and they brought our class over so they can tell the region that the beds were all full. (Misrepresentation) They delay people's halfway houses. They refuse to send people to boot camp so they can make money by keeping them here. The way they are treating us is a sin.

We are having a class on UFOs in two weeks. It is going to be a hit. Urantia talks about a planet nearby with a civilization more advanced than us. There is no evidence to substantiate life on other planets in our solar system but there are millions of planets out there. So, I plan to bust out this class with my Urantia Book. If they are in space crafts, they must be mortals because celestial personalities don't need space ships. It's going to be fun!

I got a picture from Grace and a card from both kids today. I need to write to them. Thanks for the letter. I look forward to *funny times.*

Hi, Chuck,

Mr. Hunt left today for a halfway house. I am going to miss him. He did so much for us here. He is an honorable man, and one I respect totally. He was down fifty-four months, and they never gave him a furlough. Good luck, Mr. Hunt. I don't think you will have any problems.

Here is an interesting bit of information. The question is, who was Jay Black? Do you remember "Jay and the Americans"? They had some hits back in the sixties. I was talking to my friend Bob A. (Michael Milken's lawyer). He said Jay got onto some money problems with the Howard Beach family and ended up being owned by John Gotti. Bob says he knew them both from the neighborhood. So, then I asked him about the neighbor who accidentally ran over J. G.'s kid. Bob said he lived on the other side of J. G. I stood there with my mouth open!

I probably won't be trading the OEX anymore. I am going to devote all of my time to the drug class.

It's different being in C-unit. I don't see all of the usual people. They try to isolate us from the other population. I don't see Jim at all.

I may be becoming a C-unit orderly, so I won't ever have to leave the unit.

Say hello to Jill, Kath, and Lew for me next time you see them.

Take care.

G

Letter number 108, FPC Allenwood January 22, 1997, to John Kravetz

Johnny,

Miro here, chillin' from the crack house. Here is the official word.

February 19, class begins

November 13, last class.

November 20, graduation

Any time after graduation I go to a halfway house. Just got a letter from Russel M. He was in Woodstock, Vermont, halfway house for four months. Now he is home on a bracelet.

I am getting a job in this unit as an orderly.

Still no word on J. M. My friend Brian has five more years to go.

That's the scoop for now. I am very excited about this new chapter that is about to begin.

Be cool.

MM

Dear Charlene,

Classes started today. Nothing really exciting happened yet except that I need a favor. Our teacher wants us to have a self-help meeting book sent in from the Southern Vermont area. Could you please call the NA or AA and get a book sent here for me? I have to have one to show him. Thanks a lot. I have to go to two NA or AA meetings a week starting tonight.

So we begin. I also have to take other courses along the way. I start my job search skills and career development course in March. It's worth thirty hours. I have to get fifty-five hours of class on my own along with the 450 hours that they will give me. It's going to be very interesting.

A prison bus showed up here yesterday and one again today. I watched them unload today's bus looking for my friend Brian, but he was not on board. We aren't allowed to be in the area of a bus unloading, but we can watch from the second-floor windows.

Bad news: a guy showed up here yesterday who came down on the bus from FCI Raybrook. Brian was with him, but they took him off behind the walls at Lewisburg Penitentiary! Motherfuckers put him in with all of those maniacs. Why do they hate him so much? Because he won an appeal, that's why! This guy says that Brian still has some sort of appeal for a reduction going on. What a place to wait. God, I was so excited to see him.

What happens when I get out of here? Interestingly enough, my drug class teacher told us to get with one of the councilors and let them know where I wanted to go to the halfway house. I didn't know that I had a choice. I might go someplace different if I had employment opportunities there such as in Boston. I know a lot of Boston people. Right now, my friend Moe from Springfield, Massachusetts, wants me to buy cars for him. He gets out a little before me, and his operation never shut down.

My teacher told me that he will have me in a halfway house before Thanksgiving. I should be there for six months. Russel stayed four months and went home on an electric bracelet

Well, I got to go now and deliver my Urantia presentation. I just got back. It went over pretty well.

It was very cold today, and I walked two miles with my buddy Johnny Z. from Waterville, Maine.

Boy time seems to be dragging lately and for no reason really. Being over here seems more tedious. There's really not much of a difference, but knowing that it is the last step to freedom just keeps me more on edge. The work we are required to do isn't really overwhelming but still, I am on edge. In three more weeks two of my friends will be coming over. Maybe I will settle down by then. Right now, I am flying a mile a minute.

I only work about two hours a day cleaning the bathrooms. I lift weights now. I am enjoying that. Well, I am going to take this down to the mailbox now.

Love,
Me

Johnny Boy,

Corn Bread here! My new drug counselor just walked by and told me I had a messy cube. Where is that asshole? I'm gonna kick his ass.

We are having regional inspections this week with lots of suits running around. It sucks to have to stick around with all these peckerheads.

I got this great new job working one-and-a-half hours a day in this building.

Things will be back to normal next week. I went to advanced Spanish tonight. It's been going on for three weeks. I love hanging with the Dominicans and PRs. I do a Urantia presentation next week. I have to get my ducks in a row. My friend Bryan and Jim M. are due back in April. I need some company. Hope they show.

Love,
Me

Johnny,

Greg Piccolo and Heavy Juice will be playing here on March 4th. Funky R&B sax. I can't wait to hear some live music. It's gonna be in the gym. It's gonna be hard to hear, but I gotta see this guy. It's a free concert. He probably did some time once.

Lifting is progressing nicely. I added two more exercises to my thing today and added a little more weight. I am getting pecs and bulges!

Today it was 50 degrees here and sunny. Movin', grooving, gritty, and boss!

I talked to Viola today. It was a good talk. They opened a little store in the house. Boy, do I ever miss that woman? That bitch is gonna be walking bow-legged when I get through with her!

Well, gotta go for now. Be cool my brother.

Mel

El Monk,

Ol' Mell Bell is hell when he's well, and he's hell tonight. I just came from working on my *buff!*

Time marches on. We lost one of our classmates today. He got caught bringing in a package. His girl brought it onto the reserve and the hacks staked it out. When he showed they *pounced*, and now he is in the hole. He lost his good time in the drug program. He was already down for sixty-one months. Too bad for "Bones." This reminds me of the time Charlene wore my sneakers over her tiny little shoes. She made it, all though lots of guys noticed. We had a good laugh after visiting was over!

Happy Saint Patty's Day! I called Mom today to wish her a happy and ran out of phone credits.

I halfway expect Jim M. to come walking up the path at any time. Hope he did okay. These fucking pigs, I hate 'em. I mean it. (Knuckleheads.)

I'm still counting down the days till release. I can't stop. I should try to forget the time. Another class graduates on Thursday. Another class starts in April. So now I'm a sophomore.

We had a quiz the other day. I got a 90. Cool!

You know I'm gonna study for these motherfuckers! I have to write a history of my drug use. It starts way back when I drank *tango* at the cascades, and you guys rolled me out of the car onto my parent's front lawn! That was the beginning. I won't forget to include Diana's pool *bird-a-thon* or flying across the *Provincetown dunes on acid* with Zanny and Dot! Oh, wow! And don't forget the Passa Grill "Orange Sunshine" exposé, surfing on mescaline, Laurie the teenage ball freak, Beau Arts, the out-of-sight shop, sixty-eight kinds of hash, *strawvon* snorting, amyl nitrate huffing, "Albert King," and incident in Duck's living room. I will need extra paper. I never should have hung out with you, *bad influences*. My mother was right!

The wind is blowing hard, snow tonight. Another three weeks of winter. The Canadian geese are returning. Each one shits twelve times a day, and there are thousands of them. I don't have to clean it up, but someone does. I am the C-2 dorm orderly now. I have classes all the time and work one hour a day. On November 20th, I will graduate (eight and a half months). *Stop counting, Miro!*

It's basketball fever is here, and the gamblers are tying up the phones to their bookies! I saw Fairfield U the other night, two TVs going on all the time. Baseball starts soon; forget about it in this fucking place. I am indifferent to most sports except Wiffle Ball.

Gotta go study.

Keep the faith.

Miro

Chuck,

I am starting this letter early so I don't forget some things I need to tell you. Can you please get me an NA and AA schedule? We have to get them and bring them to class. It is required. Maybe they have them at the old hospital in Bellows Falls.

I just got a letter from Bugs. He beat "Supper Fly Jimmy Snuka" (the wrestler) in a game of pool at "the Crossroads."

I spoke to my daughter, Gracie. She is going to graduate from high school in the spring. I guess I am going to miss it, but the good news is she is graduating!

Classes are in full swing now. I had my first group. We didn't do much, but we will next Friday. I had to write a history of my drug use. It was three pages long. Then I had to write a paper on how I feel when I take drugs. Then I have to write a paper on why I think I need drugs. We will discuss those in class or in the group.

Next, I have to write papers on my guilty feelings over how I fucked over my kids. That seems to be my biggest issue. Now that I have been clean and sober for almost three years, that is the issue that seems to pop up all the time. I have to make amends when I get out. That is my first priority. I miss those guys.

Thanks again for those postcards. I have been sending them out. I love the Marx Brothers cards especially

Gracie and Travis sent me an Easter Card. It is an Easter Bunny Mooning me! It's the Keister Bunny. Get it?

The NA and AA books may only be pamphlets. That is okay. Schedules of meetings are what he wants I think. I go to NA meetings. I even chaired a meeting last Friday. They are a good place to let off steam I guess. I don't talk much to them so last Saturday, they asked me why so I told them that on April 4th, I would be clean for three years the reason being that I have been locked up. I can't have drugs in here so it makes it easier to abstain. I feel very free with no pressure to get loaded. I know there are drugs here, but I think this time, I really want to stop. On the street, it might be different.

NA meetings are maintenance for me when I feel the urges. In here, urges are not as strong after three years of sobriety. Plus, I am doing all of this other work on my drug and psychological problems. So I go because it is required, and I share if I have something to share. But sometimes, most times I don't have much to say. Speaking of which, I have to go to rational recovery right now. I will write more later. I'm back. I don't know if I like R. R. I need fifteen hours of it so I gotta keep going. It is only in the other room. Tomorrow I start job search skills. My resume is going to look really good. Previous job, coke dealer. I guess it is time to start a legal business. At least I know that *I* will hire me.

So you got all dressed up in a skirt and heels. Oh, baby! Congratulations on winning in court. Cops are such assholes.

I think I will come back to Vermont for starters. I want to be near the kids. I need to reconnect. After that, we will see what takes place. I gotta go now.

Love,
Mel

J. K.,

Cool, 'sup, keed? Still chillin'! It's a beautiful day here. I walked three miles and did crunches for an hour. Tonight we are having an outside basketball team come in to play the Allenwood All-Stars. I don't know their name. I think it's the Oxbow Reefers! I cannot attend as I am guest chair at a NA meeting. So I got that going for me.

So you got a visit from S. S. T. Fuck her. She should keep her mouth shut. I don't know nothing. The feds taught me that.

You sent me two letters, and I haven't had one letter from Charlene. I wonder if she is okay. Maybe I will call if I don't hear something soon.

Nicolas Cage movies. *Birdie*, yes I saw that one. It was excellent. No, I never saw *Red Rock West*. Tell Balinda she has good taste in movies.

Greetings to all, Igor, V'mon, Suzette, JR, and Suzzy F.

Bugs and Grace are getting ready to make the trip down to Camp Allenwood. I can't wait to see the face in the place.

It should be good.

You still got IRS troubles? Hey, I know a couple of accountants in here that could dazzle them with Bullshit! Scumbags.

Well, I gotta go do my NA thing.

Love,
Lamar Zoot

Miro here.

I just got back from the library. I have been spending time with my sexy new job search skills instructor. "Hey, babe you got a great ass." She is trying to get me rehabilitated with a great job training program. So what do I wanna be? I told her about the job I had in a hobby horse factory punching out assholes! She said that doesn't count. It ain't easy finding a job when you are fifty, especially in Vermont. I am sending resumes to some addresses she gave me. I really just want to get in her pants. Lack o' nookie makes you crazy!

The weather was beautiful here today. It's almost time for the Canadian geese to return. Only a few have shown up so far. The boys are gearing up for the poop patrol! They should be flocking in here any time soon. Get those brushes and buckets ready. Them dirty fuckin' birds!

I went to the team today. They are sending me to Vermont for a halfway house. It turns out, Vermont has no federal halfway houses, so I went to Boston. That sucks for us Vermonters because we have to get another job and housing after we leave here.

Well, dude, keep in touch. Now I have to write another report. So I gotta go

Love and kisses,
Gazza Balloons and the Prunes

Letter number 116, FPC Allenwood, April 2, 1997, to Charlene Wakefield

Charlene,

I got your postcard a few days ago. I am excited about the visit. I haven't had one since last summer.

Today in class, our DAP counselor was talking about Doe and Ti. You know the ones who committed suicide so that they could go to heaven on a spaceship. So he asked the class if any of us were members of *heaven's gate*. We all said no. So after class, my latest Urantia book student tells him about the U book. Next thing I know I get called into Mr. Salvatore's office. He wants to see the book. I wrote a *wellness* paper on that saying in the U book about using "Our Father" in prayer. I told him to read it. The paper compares Jesus's early home life with modern-day children's. If he reads that paper, he should get a little glimpse.

That wonderful woman from Fargo, Frances McDormand, is married to one of the Coen brothers and has been in many of their movies. I think I have seen 90 percent of them. Willian H. Macy went to school with Lynn and stole my first love away from me. Then he divorced her. She lives in Vermont now. Her name is Becky. I don't know her last name now.

It would be very nice if you could attend Gracie's graduation. I really wanted to be there.

Well, I have to go to a job search skills class now. It's a six-week class, and I can't wait till it is over. We are only in the second week.

Gotta go now.

Love,
G

J. K. Johnny Boy,

'Sup, dude? Got a letter from Will C. telling me he had J. M.'s address in the Texas joint, but he didn't give it to me.

Charlene was here last weekend. It was an excellent visit. She brought me Cadbury eggs.

Its' neck and neck in the letter-writing heat. Each of you writes once a week, and I look forward to them all.

I am tacking a shit load of courses and job search skills. They want to know what I want to be when I grow up. Group therapy, drug class, AA, NA, and national recovery.

Marshal Applewhite, alias "Doe," and his wife "Ti" left without me. I wanted to know whether I should change my name to Fa, So, La, or Re. Give me some of that electric Kool-Aid and gad the colors! What do you know about that Ancient Dominican city good tourist thang? Maybe I will go down and sell T-shirts.

Some local college basketball team came here yesterday and proceeded to kick the shit out of the "Allenwood All-Stars." Good, they suck, and they take up too much gym time.

The weather has been pretty good though still too fucking windy for me. The sun is out. Daylight savings is in, and I am still fucking here. November 20 is graduation, but who's counting.

I am still crunching and lifting. I am eating too much though. I gotta stop now. I am spinning my wheels in the dieting department.

Well that's all folks.

Peace on ya!

Love,
Miro

Hi, Chuck,

Glad you made it home safe. It's a long ride. Thanks for Angelo and Diane's address, but I don't feel the urge to write. Willy wrote me a postcard saying he had J. M.'s address but he didn't give it to me. Fuck it. Hey, great visit. Thanks for the chocolate and for letting me *feel you up*. It was much appreciated!

So Kravetz and Marielle are going to be on Candid Camera. That should be interesting.

I got a new barber, and he wanted to know about the Urantia book. I owe him two tins of fish so I am going to bring them to him tonight and give him some info about the U book.

I went to see Dr. Findley. He is the head shrink here. He gave me a psychological profile test a couple of weeks ago, and I went in to find the results. He said that I was more normal than 98 percent of the inmates here, but I was not a regular guy in terms of society. He said I was a little *unconventional*. He said that was good, but I needed to find something to do, and then the sky's the limit. I scored a little high on anxiety. I have to work on that one. That will probably go away once I get a job and settle in. I also have done more drugs than anyone else on the compound. Thank you very much, ladies and gentlemen!

Well, gotta go. Keep those cards and letters coming in. I read them all.

Mel

Kravetz,

No class for me today. Half the other guys in the class did poorly on the first test we had, so the ones who passed got a couple of classes off. I have a group at ten then I am done for the weekend.

Today is freezing and very windy with snowflakes, and George is getting *upset*! Just kidding.

I am in the calisthenics class now, also I am crunching up a storm. Today is weights day. I am going down at 12:00 and doing a nice slow workout. I went up five pounds on all of my exercises. I am pumped up!

This is the eighth week of my drug program. I got two months in and only seven more to go.

The weather is still cold and shitty, but the forecast calls for 60 degrees tomorrow. So I guess I won't be trying to catch Hale-Bopp. I had my new Reeboks, Kool-Aid, and plastic bag ready to go.

Charlene sent me some postcards of James Brown, a.k.a. The Godfather, on the good foot. "Baby, take my hand. I wanna be your loving man. Oh, oh, oh, I love you so."

Gotta go till next time.

Miro

Letter number 120, FPC Allenwood, May 4, 1997, to Charlene Wakefield

Hi, Chuck,

I saw Kravetz on *Candid Camera*. He was on for all of ten seconds! He needs to get out more often. He didn't know they ate pancakes in California!

I am starting this letter early because I got some good news yesterday. They are going to allow us dope dealers to apply for furloughs. One friend of mine has already gotten one. I have my next team meeting in five weeks, and that is where I can apply. That would be nice to get together for a while. It's premature, but I still can't help getting excited.

My friend Mac is showing me how to acquire preexisting businesses. That is what he did on the outside. He wants to get a feel for what is out there in our area so could you send me some classified sections from our area.

Also, could you send me a graduation card for Gracie? That is one card that I would find hard to get in here. My baby is graduating high school. Wow!

Well, gotta go. Write soon.

G

Letter number 121

I got this letter from a recently released fellow inmate from Vermont telling me about the halfway house in Windsor, Vermont. His name is Jonah.

Hey, George,

Here are the answers to your questions. Sorry, it took so long.

While you are at Woodstock, you don't have to pay anything (unlike Boston where I ended up). You can get home and get out pretty much whenever you want and as soon as you want. The day after I got there, I got an all-day pass to Brattleboro, Vermont.

I had a twelve-hour layover in White River, Vermont. So I got a motel room and spent the night. It is only 20 miles from Woodstock. It was a long ride from Pennsylvania though. Eighteen hours with layovers in New York City and Boston. South Station has everything, mini restaurants bookstores, and hookers!

Tell your caseworker that you need money for the trip and motel room because the bus station in White River closes at eleven. You get off the bus at around 12:00 p.m. That leaves plenty of time to get rested or whatever. You will have to report to Woodstock by like 11:00 a.m. the next day. That would be the best thing to do I think.

Send all your stuff home because you don't want to carry it with you. I had two boxes of stuff on my trip and it was a *bitch*. Send it home, man! If there is anything else I can do, drop me a line.

Later.

Jonah

Hey, Doc,

Well, bro, it's almost over. What a long strange trip it's been. Soon you will be free and you deserve it.

I'm anxious to meet your new love. I am putting her telephone number on my list and will be calling you once I know you are there. Are you going back to Florida?

Things here are the same. It sucks. The drug program is going along as usual. I have six and a half months left till halfway house. These people have been dragging their feet getting the program up and running. They are always shy one teacher. Delay tactics because the camp population is down. They gotta get that tuition. Some inmates have taken them to court.

We all have next week off on account that it is no big deal to complete the program. You can do it in three months. So why is it taking nine months? These people are miserable fucks, and if I could fuck them without fucking myself, I'd do it in a heartbeat! I am getting five months off my sentence instead of twelve and six months in a halfway house. The next group is only getting three months. My DTS says he will have us in a halfway house by November 21. In my case, it will be in Woodstock, Vermont. I tried to get to Boston, but they said no because I had no ties there. (Such liars. I ended up in Boston.) It doesn't matter because nothing is gonna stop me from flying once I get out. I'm gonna step up to big pay. I have learned a lot here from these wiz-kid inmates surrounding me. Gonna do some *world shakin'* soon brother. Maybe we can do some together! It won't be the first time.

I have been in the weight room and am getting a little shape. I hurt myself badly the first time I went ten months ago. Now it feels much better, and I have a couple of guys coaching me.

So keep in touch, Doc. This chapter is almost over. I know this book will have a happy ending.

Keep the faith.
George

Hi, Chuck,

I saw Kravetz on *Candid Camera* for all of ten seconds, but it was neat! He has got to get out more. He didn't know they ate pancakes in California!

We got some good news or at least a good rumor. They are supposedly going to allow drug class inmates to apply for furloughs. One guy already got one but I am not holding my breath.

No classes this week because my teacher is being sued by an inmate for fucking with his time off. These guys here have to learn that they are not God, and they can't keep screwing with us just because their census is low. You could complete this program in four months, so we aren't worried about falling behind.

No, I didn't see the diving horse when I was a kid. But my uncle George had home movies of it from his Atlantic City vacation. It was very cool. We all loved the postcard. We love all of your cards.

I hope we get *Sling Blade* next. They won't let us have *R*-rated flicks anymore, so we send them to a company that edits movies for the airlines, and they never return them on time.

Thanks for the Urantia book info. It is all welcome. I will have time to read it this week since I won't have class.

I hope you got your Dali prints. He is very cool. I like his stuff.

Love,
George

Thanks for the diving horse. I think the dish angel is exquisite. You are so clever, my dear.

So Doc is almost a free man. That's great. I am right behind him. I got seven months left till halfway house. Go, Georgie, go.

The program is progressing at a snail's pace. After all, it could be done in four months. Tomorrow we have a community with all of the classes together. We have a poem to read. Lameness all around! I suggested that we sing that Ringo Starr song, "No, no, no, I don't do it no more." Nobody wanted to do it so I shut up. I was afraid they might make me do it alone. My teacher hates this shit, but it is his boss (Dr. Findlay). That does. This place is full of *wackos*. And that is just the staff!

That's great news about Doc. He sounds great. He is almost free at last. I love the poster. They won't let us use the computers here, the scumbags. All they do here is force the guys to get their GEDs. They get $3,000 for each inmate to complete the course. The inmate probably gets a cookie!

Gracie got me an AA schedule from Parks Place. That is all I need to satisfy my DTS (drug treatment specialist). He is happy now.

Tomorrow night, I chair my first AA meeting. I will do it for two months.

Gotta go now. Thanks for all of the letters.

Love,
George

I'm just back from watching Seinfeld. It's on here five days a week at five thirty. We have a club (Jerry's kids). Tonight was the farting-horse, marble-rye, Elaine's sax-playing boyfriend who won't eat her pussy. I have seen them all, but they still make me laugh especially here.

So how come I get two letters from you at once? You got the *mean woman blues*? That same thang that makes a tomcat howl all night. I ain't seen my main squeeze in three long years today. You know I got the blues!

I've been thinking about some of the old gangs and how they are doing. Mike hit the halfway house on June 7th. What a long strange trip it's been?

Miro

Johnny Boy,

Thanks for the jokes. I got a letter from Bugs and Grace today. They are coming to visit the first week in June. Great. Maybe by then, it will have warmed up. It has been windy and freezing for weeks. Bugs sent me the schedule and list of groups for the New Orleans Jazz Festival. The lineup is intense.

I finally got back into the weight room with some big-time bodybuilders. I am getting a mondo—intense workout together and my shoulder feels great. I am getting pumped up, no more girlie man!

I got another week off from class. My teacher and Dr. Findlay (program head) are being sued by an inmate for denying him his year off. They are gonna lose big time. Man, these assholes have been playing God with too many people's lives. Fuck 'em where they breathe!

Only six and a half months to go in this hellhole. I'm ready. Ready as anybody can be. I'm ready for you. I hope you're ready for me.

We have giant greenhouses and gardens here. All the inmates who work there make big bucks selling produce to the guys who don't eat in the cafeteria. I like my one-and-a-half-hour a day job. No money but plenty of time to work out. I didn't come to the jail to work. All you can buy is junk food and cigarettes. Give me a healthy life. I gotta go to rational recovery now.

Love and kisses,
Your pal, Ziggaboo Modeliste

Dear Charlene,

It's freezing cold here, and last night the wind knocked a tree over. It's more like March 21 than May 21. It's driving us all nuts!

The drug class is going along slowly but surely. We got another confirmation on the November 21 release date. It looks good. We had a test yesterday, and I did fine. That was my third test.

I got a letter from Marilyn yesterday. Brian is at the low or medium down the road. I don't know for sure, but he has met some people that know me from here. That tells me that she is at a low-security facility. About a year ago they took all of the illegal aliens out of here and put them behind a fence when the INS laws changed. I don't think I know anyone at the FCI or medium security. I wrote Brian a letter asking him who he met.

Only six months till halfway house. I am excited as hell thinking about it.

Tonight is the start of the *everything-you-always-wanted-to-know-about-cigars* class. I am not going because a friend of mine is developing a self-improvement, maximum achievement class. He is trying it out on some of us under the guise of an AA meeting. It's fun. I am reading a book called *Maximum Achievement.* I have read a couple of others, Napoleon Hill and Norman Vincent Peale, but this guy is much more detailed. Besides I will get credit for another AA meeting. I got all of the extra courses that I needed on my own. I have completed two treatment plans and am waiting for my third. I don't what he will have me take. Shame and guilt sound interesting, also criminal lifestyles. We shall see now that my job search skills class is over. I have the whole afternoon to myself, and I will spend it lifting weights. I am going to put something legal together when released. I can smell it!

I talked to Travis and Grace yesterday. It has been a long time. They made me feel better.

What is the exact date of Gracie's graduation? I will definitely mention that you got it for me and thank you again. I love it.

It is finally nice out. It rained for three days. Nice place for a prison.

Did I tell you that a blind guy I met in here had me send for a Urantia book tape so he could listen? I can't wait for it to come so I can listen to him. I just got a reply from the Morning Star Foundation. I thought that they had tapes, but they only have booklets written by this one guy who heads the new foundation. There are too many foundations for me. Besides all of the information, that you sent me from Joan Neuman is the best. It's from Dr. Sadler. He is one of the original U dudes. I think I will stick with him.

Thank you so much for the letter. I will try to give you a call soon. Take care.

George

Johnny,

Well, this is the last Memorial Day weekend that I will be spending in this shit hole! So I got that going for me, which is good! Burgers and dogs and rock 'n' roll don't mean shit without some female companionship. That's what I always say, "Gimme a pig foot and a gang of gin! Check all your razors and your guns. We gonna be wrestlin' when the wagon comes!"

The weather finally broke today. That's not to say it won't be cold again tomorrow. I finally met a guy in here who like me gets nervous when the wind blows! See, I ain't crazy after all.

I have got to go chair an AA meeting right now. I will write more later. There that's over with. They are showing a Stallone movie right now. So between that and the baseball game, nobody comes to the AA meeting, which is okay with me.

How about Frank Gifford getting it *wet* on the side! Kathy Lee will cut off his balls! He's a freak at the freaker's ball.

Gotta go.

Your pal,
Corn Bread

J. K.,

Well, I was headed down the walking trail today when I heard some-one calling my name. I turned around and it was J. M. It was great to see him. We walked three miles and had dinner together. They mis-takenly sent him to an FCI. That's a regular prison with real convicts doing a hard time. He said that in the two months he was there, he got into five beefs. He stayed in his cell a lot, but he is safe back here now. He looks good, and they can't keep him here any longer than March. He could be out as soon as December. So it is almost over for both of us.

Next week is my birthday and hopefully, Bugs and Grace will pay a visit. I'd love to see them. My kids sent me a really intense birthday card. I laughed my ass off!

I saw a video last week called "Inside Rikers Island," 24,000. Count 'em, inmates. They have shootings in there. There is a gay wing and an AIDS wing. So you see it could be a lot worse.

See ya.

Love,
Corn Bread

Hi, Charlene,

Got the results of my last two tests back yesterday, and they were both excellent. That's three tests and three excellent. I must be an excellent guy!

Just saw *Star Trek: First Contact.* Very boring. Also Stallone's tunnel movie is also a big snore.

Then I went to NA, AA group counselor meeting, long and drawn-out boring meeting. I asked Joe Waldholtz if he was crazy for wanting to have a career in politics, and he said, "Now you know why I took drugs." Holly shit what a pain in the ass this group is. I am quitting at the end of June.

Those *Funny Times* magazines you send are great. Two of us got articles for our "wellness" papers out of there. I love it.

I had another test today and another excellent score! Isn't that excellent?

Jim has to go through orientation all over again. He was trying to find a job before he gets put in food service or on the bus to the *low* or *medium.* I took him over to see my boss in laundry, and he got hired!

Bugs and Grace are supposed to come for a visit this weekend. I hope they do.

It has been really cold lately. Today was a little better.

My mom sent me fifty dollars for my birthday so I splurged and bought myself a pair of weight-lifting gloves. They really help. I'm really living it up out here on the reservation. The warden found out that the inmates have been maintaining the weight machines so the asshole confiscated the cables. They are phasing out the weight rooms because the inmates are intimidating the guards so when something breaks, they won't replace it. This warden is some special brand of shit.

Brian is at the low. I hope he gets transferred here. Maybe he will after six months or so once they see he will be no trouble.

I am glad that Ellen is getting rid of that loser. Lots of guys in prison try to play women like that. She probably sent him money. Guys in here, especially the young ones, write to two or three girls at a time on the outside. The girls send them sneakers and phone credits. I hear them talking all day long.

Well, that's all for now. It was a very nice letter you sent. I'm going to mail this letter right now.

G

Hey, baby,

Well, I'm a happy guy this week. I finally found a diet that works! It's not a new diet; it's the Scarsdale diet. You cut out the starch and get all of your carbs from veggies and fruit. Forget about calories, even eat a bit of fat. I have been on it now for eight days and lost seven pounds. I'm excited. I'm turning into a regular Vic Tanny.

Well, there's only one thing around here that changes more than the weather and that's BOP policy. My new halfway house date is October 30, and Woodstock, Vermont, is only taking female federal inmates. So I could go to Boston after all or maybe even Rutland. I'll keep you posted. Mort gets out at the same time. He told them he wanted Woodstock and said that he would refuse halfway period if they tried to send him to Concord. Concord is under investigation for corruption so he may end up in Boston. Like I said every day is something new. I still think we may be released sooner. They are putting in another class so that's good for the guys who are waiting.

My buddy Rob just got some good news. They have five days to release him. He was supposed to go home after he graduated from DAP class in July, but they said that he had enhancements so Rob took these assholes to court and won. He can sue and get $375.00 for every day he was kept over. That's a nice settlement.

Doc is in Tampa. I haven't put his telephone *number* on my list yet.

I got a graduation announcement from Gracie. Wish I could be there.

I got my application from the State of Vermont to apply for vocational training. I may get some free training. I have to check when I get out.

Well, I gotta go put this in the mail so it goes out tomorrow.

Love,
G

Shonny,

Yo brother from anutha mutha still chillin' on the home skillet.

Bugs and Grace never made it. I listened for a page all week-end. So my new story is this. Remember, you can't tell the players without a score card. I am now going to be in a halfway house on October 30, but Woodstock, Vermont, is not taking any male federal inmates right now. Now there is talk of Rutland, Vermont, or Boston, Massachusetts. The feds will not send anyone to Concord, New Hampshire, halfway which by the way is the prison because of a corruption scandal.

Jim M. and I leave the same month. He will be going to Boston. I may even get out earlier than October 30th, but that's where it stands right now.

Spanish is coming along pretty well. My Dominican friends here started a conversation club every Monday for an hour. I learn a lot there.

I have to go right now. *Seinfeld* is coming on. I am one of Jerry's kids! I'm back. I was the famous Sponge episode!

I am eligible for vocational training from the State of Vermont when I get out. I can maybe get computer training.

Doc is out and in a Tampa, Florida, halfway house.

Well, be cool. Can't wait to see you.

Arturo Sandoval

Letter number 133, FPC Allenwood, June 19, 1997, to Charlene Wakefield

Dear Charlene,

My daughter, Grace, graduates from high school tonight. I talked to her and her brother Travis today. Take some pictures for me. Okay? I am so proud of her.

Speaking of pictures, don't bother sending any more postcards. These assholes called me into the mail room today. They had two that I sent out to Owl and Bugs (they didn't send them), and they had your letter that I got today. They confiscated two postcards that you just sent (you sent three, they missed one, "The Phantom of the Opera." They said that postcards are unauthorized stationery. New rules. I have twenty of them in my locker that you assholes let in over the past thirty months. These people never fail to amaze me. Anyway, I can't send them now so hold off on them, please. Thank you.

October 30, 1997, yes that is the day I leave: October 30, 1998 is my out date. So I will get six plus six. Six months off and six months in a halfway house. I will take it. Now if they could just find me a place to go I will be happy.

I spoke to one guy from Manchester, New Hampshire, who leaves in August, and he is going to Boston. No one is being sent to Concord so that corruption rumor must be true. So if Vermont is not taking any federal inmates, I could end up in Boston which would be okay. I am just gonna leave it up to fate. I am tired of second-guessing. I will do well wherever I go. Just let me out. *Now.* My drug treatment specialist is trying to figure out if the Urantia Book is a cult. I gave him the *History of the Movement* paper to read. He wants to believe, but he is such a cop sometimes. I told him that in five hundred years, the U book would be the new bible on this planet. Sometimes I wonder if I should be sharing this stuff with him. It's so boring in here. I like to stir things up! So the river of shit flows on.

Well, baby, I hope the graduation was fun. I am going to go mail this now so that it goes out tomorrow.

Love,
G

Kravetz,

Nobody messes with Red Dalton's girl, and Injun Joe is ticklish!

Yes, I remember CC, and I saw her a few times when I was locked up in Westmoreland, New Hampshire. She had a client there with me.

Bugs sent me a card saying that he and Owl would be down soon. Charlene may bring my kids down too. I am applying for a furlough so maybe I can get laid.

October 30th, and I should be gone from here. I still don't know where: Boston, or Rutland, Vermont, who knows.

I spoke to Gracie and Travis yesterday. I told Gracie how proud I was of her. Travis is still doing *drive-bys* (just kidding). I will be back in his life real soon.

Two days ago, I ran five miles. It wasn't that hard. It gets easier the more I do it. I am going to try for six miles on Sunday. I lost eleven pounds in sixteen days. I now weigh 193 pounds. I now take fourteen days on a maintenance diet and do it all again. I will be looking good by the time I get out. I owe it to the women, you know. They have been waiting so patiently!

I got busted by the mail room for sending dirty postcards. They said I couldn't have them. So how come you assholes let thirty of them through? Fucking cops. I really hate them now.

Gotta go to my AA meeting.

Love,
"Busta" Rhymes

Dear Charlene,

I got a picture of Grace in her cap and gown and also a picture of Travis. He is thinning out and growing taller. He looks good. If only he would go to school. I like his haircut.

It is true that we aren't allowed to associate with other felons, but there is really no way for them to catch us unless they caught us doing a crime together. I wouldn't make too much out of it.

It would really be great if they had a halfway house in Brattleboro, Vermont. My counselor, Mr. Defrancisco, is the one who finds bed space for us in halfways all over the country. I am going to see him on Monday. I really need to know where he is going to send me. I want to start making plans. This guy Moe wants to have me buy cars for him. He gets out in October. If I am going to Vermont, I can work for him. If I am going to Boston I know some people who might help me get started.

Good for your daughter Asia making the dean's list. I wish Travis would make some list! He will find something. He just has no direction.

On a side note, today, Travis is doing great. He is a realtor and owns apartment houses. That's my boy!

It's Friday night, and I just did my final AA chair meeting. That info can go into my central file. That info will get me a Snickers bar.

Our teacher left on a three-week vacation so we get three weeks off. That is another ploy to keep us here longer. It's all a part of the government's fleecing of America. No one fucks the taxpayers as well as the Bureau of Prisons. Only four months to go. I never thought it would come.

Well, baby, that's about all from here for now. I am still proceeding at a steady rate, slow. Soon this will all be a memory.

All my love,
G

Letter number 136, FPC Allenwood, July 3, 1997 to Johnny Kravetz

J. K.,

The July 4th weekend is just starting up. My teacher is still on vacation, so I have nothing to do. I get through work at 9:00 a.m., and the rest of the day I am free.

I ran ten miles, yes ten miles, two days ago to win a bet I had with another guy. So now he has to run two miles a day for thirty days. I am not going to try to increase the amount I am running. I am going to start running five miles three days a week. I am glad that I did it though. I am still lifting five days a week. That's enough exercise.

Tomorrow there is a major feast for the 4th with T-bones, burgers, and dogs but no women. Bummer.

The Ben and Jerrys concert sounds great. Charlene went to see 10,000 Maniacs, but Natalie Merchant is no longer with the group. I could use some live music. We are having some tomorrow, but no one is really very good.

I went to my team meeting and was denied a furlough. They said I was too short on time. I never really expected one.

Vermont isn't taking any federal inmates halfway right now so I may end up in Boston.

It sucks to get halfway far from home because once you are done, you have to do it all over again. Say I go to Boston, get a job, and save some money. Don't bother getting an apartment because as soon as I am sent home, I will need to get another job and a place to live in Vermont.

I know some people from Boston whom I met here. That may or may not be healthy for me.

We have lots of movies for the weekend which is good because the boredom could be awful.

Say hello to Big Brad and Sweet Lorraine for me.

See ya man.
Corn Bread Red

Well, it's the July 4th weekend. We got lots going on, but I am doing business as usual. I may go to BBQ and see a movie.

Halfway house news is that Vermont has no room for federal inmates. They are clogging up Vermont jails. I said yes to Coolidge house in Boston, but that means nothing. They need to build a federal facility in Vermont. I said no to Lawrence, Massachusetts. But that doesn't mean they won't send me there.

My two friends in here are getting out at the same time as me are working on some business plan. They want to include me, but I don't know because I am not allowed to associate with other felons.

My friend Jerry finally got his Urantia Book. It is from the Foundation, and it cost $20.00. It has concentric circles and a flexible plastic cover. I got a couple more people interested, and I gave them some information. My friend Johnny Z had his sister send one for him. So now I can get my copy back. There is a blind guy in here who got the audio tapes. He invited me over for a listen. I will go soon.

When I got the news that my friend Stacy is dying, I was very upset. I got a counselor here to give me an emergency phone call. She picked up the phone, and we talked for fifteen minutes. She has seen two doctors and has been given two to six months to live. She has not given up and has another appointment with a third doctor. My ex Susan has spoken to her about the Urantia Book and told her that she would be seeing Nebadon. I told her the same thing and sent her the paper about the First mansion world where you get to look up people you knew on Earth. I hope it's a comfort to her. That kid could never catch a break. It's so sad.

Well gotta go now.

Love,
Me

Shonny Boy,

Got a letter from Charlene yesterday with pictures of Gracie's graduation and also some pictures of Travis' and Laima's family.

Another Vermont guy who went out on a writ at the same time as Jim M. came back yesterday. He said they put them on Con Air and flew them down to El Reno, Oklahoma. There they put Jim into the Big House and flew him (Roger) up to Vermont. He was up there for three weeks for retrial then yesterday they took him to Manchester, New Hampshire, to put him back on the plane for here. As he was getting on the plane Jim M. was getting off. So he just got to New Hampshire. He said he thought they were going to take him to Middlebury, Vermont.

I had my team meeting, and there are no contracts with Vermont for federal halfway space. So I said, "Okay, you can send me to Boston." They said they would if nothing turned up in Vermont.

On July 4th, we had a band from Baltimore called Front Door. They played Jazz and soul. Black keyboard player, West Indian Sax, soul sister on vocals, and a white chick on drums. She was intense. You couldn't even see her hands. Intense! They had a Gloria Estefan video concert on in the gym through nice big speakers

Well, I have a NA meeting now, so see ya.

Love,
Corn Bread

J. K.,

Got a new pen today. All government pens are now contraband, so I got one over at the commissary except I stole it. I am a convicted felon, you know!

I got a letter from Charlene tonight. She got a letter from Doc. He is still halfway house. He is working as a telemarketer somewhere. He wants me to write to him. I will this weekend. Bugs and Owl will be here this coming weekend. I am looking forward to that.

It's been hotter than hell here. Heat makes it hard to run. Tomorrow is Saturday, so I can run in the morning. I will run five miles. Lifting is also harder in the heat. Softball is hazardous to your health. Two guys broke legs last week. Both are in the drug class, and you can't go to halfway house if you can't work.

We got three months to go now. October 30th or maybe sooner.

We are getting ready for graduation. I have to read something in front of the crowd. It will be fun. Our teacher wants it to last fifteen minutes, and that's fine with us. Give me my diploma and a piece of cake then I'm out of here.

The Bugman and Owl visit is just what I need. Take care.

Miro

The big letter you sent. Great story about Itchy and Fish!

It has been unbearably hot here this past week. It is hard to sleep and working out is twice as hard. Tomorrow is Saturday and I will run five miles before it gets too hot.

So you heard from Doc. I will write to him soon. I don't have the phone number on my list. I should have it on when I added Stacy's. I didn't think. My unit manager will get pissed. These lazy fucks don't like to do anything but shine leather seats with their asses! Now that I have the address I will write.

I called Stacy today. She was better than the first time, but they don't give her much hope. Cancer sucks. She said that Beau lost all of his good time for fighting at Bradford or maybe at the low, so he has more like two years left to go. He is probably trying to stay longer. He was so into being an inmate when we were at FCC Raybrook. It's good that he and his brother are there together.

Vermont has a problem with halfway houses for federal detainees because they need the space for their inmates. That's why I got bounced around whenever they got filled up. They started putting inmates into apartments and when the cops checked they found girlfriends and contraband. I don't know why they won't give me one! Kids would be closer and that would be great.

This week I asked to go to Vermont, and they said no, so I took Boston.

I can't have a furlough because I am too short timewise. They come up with new rules at the drop of a hat. I had dreams of spending the night with you.

They still may shorten the program a bit, but the class in front of us complained because they won't get a reduction. Some of them threatened to call their congressmen. Right now the people who are running the program are being sued for throwing an inmate out wrongfully. While they were in court, it was revealed that Dr. Findlay, our program director, never really bothered to get his doctorate! He lied and said he wasn't allowed to shorten the classes so when Region (prison management) showed up here, they asked why our classes to nine months to complete when everyone else completed them in six months. This is a very tense place to be right now. They are looking for any excuse to throw us out. I just got rid of all unauthorized contraband. I want to be so clean that I squeak! I'm not giving them any excuse to fuck with me. This boy has had enough of jail. There won't be the next time.

Well, this is a long letter, so I will end now.

Love,
George

Psycho-Schematic Alakazam,

You're the victim, Johnny boy! Well, Owl and Bugs made it down on Saturday. It was an excellent visit. We had a great time, and it was over before I knew it. That's the last time they will visit because I ain't gonna be here motherfucker!

J. M. just got back two days ago and is back in the laundry. I still don't know where I am going to halfway house. Another guy is going to St. Johnsbury, Vermont. I don't care anymore. Maybe I will go live with Bugs. I am invited.

It's very hot and humid. The fans aren't doing shit. It just started raining so that will help.

Thank you Melinda for your article. Fortunately this place is nothing like San Quentin.

They are putting a new roof on, and the place is soaked! Fortunately my bed has been spared. My neighbor's cube is soaked. They have a hillbilly roofer chic on the crew and we all love her! There are 300 guys outside watching her use tools! It's tool time baby. "You're a tramp, honey." Bark like a dog for me! The bitch must pay. Ah, that's a shame. Treat me like the pig that I am!

I went to the gym today and bench pressed 135 pounds four times. I am a beast.

The gym is closed tomorrow. I will do some running. It's Monday, but I didn't get my *People Magazine*. Also no letter from Charlene. Tomorrow is another day.

Live it up. Have a bud.
Mel

Dear Charlene,

Finally got your letter. Thanks.

I think both Birdie and Gail are in jail. I know Birdie is. I will ask J. M. He is okay. He should be out just after me. We may both be together in halfway house.

I signed my halfway papers yesterday. They will try for Vermont first if not Boston. J. M. wants Vermont too but probably won't get it. I'm undecided. I could have picked Boston, but I really want to spend some time with the kids. Vermont will make that easier. My Boston friends won't be able to do anything till after halfway house. Boston is very crowded also so I will let the chips fall where they may.

George B. knows about this Grand Jury business. I hope he is smart enough to save his money and use their lawyers. He should take a plea and stash his cash. So now George knows, and I don't have to worry about getting in trouble for telling him. Jim will be glad to know that George isn't mad at him.

Well, it's August 1. Another month bites the dust. We are now under ninety days. Yahoo. I know that thinking about going home makes the time go slower, but I can't help it. Besides anytime I am with my classmates, that's all we think about. Some of them already have confirmation of where they are going and the date they are leaving.

Birdy is in the Middlebury, Vermont jail and Gail is in Johnson City, Texas. She is not locked up. J. M. says Birdy is scared, but he doesn't have to be as cooperative as he is being. Birdy has only been locked up for about two months now, and he is not having fun. Once it is over, he will be sent back to Bastrop, Texas. It is a low-security joint. The amount of time he gets will depend on how much he cooperates. Birdie got three years.

Lynn M. is coming down on August 14. The feds told Birdie that if he set up a deal with George and company that he would be home by Christmas.

Gotta go.

Love,
G

Nothing really new. I have been working out as usual. There is not much else to do. It is a good thing to do. It helps keep me sane.

I got a letter from Willie. He is the blues. I feel freer than him sometimes.

Your minister, Sandra, is into the Urantia book. That is very cool. You should do a reading with her. I would like to meet her someday. Maybe I should send her a copy of *The history of the Urantia Movement.*

If I get a halfway house in it won't be in St. J. Boston would be closer. I'm getting tired of trying to guess.

J. M. got a postcard from Willy today. Speaking of postcards. I love them as you know so send us some California cards to your jailbird friends from your trip. Sat hi to Mike and Asia.

My friend John Z had his sister send him a Urantia book. It was rejected, so I had him tell his counselor. I had already spent an hour in my counselor's office showing and telling. His counselor told him to send it to him. So now we have three copies here. People are burrowing my copy all the time. You should see it. Places are marked all through the old copy. I let people take it for an hour at a time! Another black friend Bob C is crazy about it and has been telling all his Baptist friends about it. One guy wants to buy my copy when I leave, but I am too attached to it to let it go. Besides I have passages marked all through it. Let's face it, the U book is the shit!

Don't send me anything more to read. They will only send it back. We have a lot of new and tighter rules. We have a new super-asshole associate warden. I refuse to even look at some of these people. I am just counting the days. I think about eleven weeks left.

Say hello to Lew, Kath, Clover, and Cliff, and everyone else.

Take care.

G

Hi, Chuck,

I don't know how long Birdie will be in Middlebury, Vermont, or even if he is still there. I don't think that Jim would know either. I just had dinner with him. He is starting his prerelease classes for the second time. I haven't done very much of mine yet. They say we drug unit don't have to because we get a good dose of it in a regular class.

The *Funny Times* magazine is great. It has such great stuff about the tobacco industry. Dr. Findlay *our administrator* has a smoking cessation class. I cut out a cartoon from *Funny Times*. People are always putting up cartoons that promote smoking pot. They always get torn down. So I put this cartoon up where the tobacco guys are at a board meeting discussing the billions of dollars in fines they have to pay. They say they have to pass the fines on to the customers because they are addicts. Instead of tearing it down, he had it framed.

Well, I'm gonna pop this one in the mail now. Have a nice trip. Say hello to me.

Love,
George

Dear Charlene,

One more week to go in August. They still haven't mailed my half-way house papers out. I think I have to sign them tomorrow. I hope I do anyway.

I decided to take a car-buying job with Moe after halfway house. I will be back in the area at least for starters. All I can think about is getting out of here.

Lynn came down last weekend with some of the kids. Jim says she wants to come down again, so they can talk. I think she wants to ask you to come along. I wish I knew exactly where I am going so that I can arrange transportation.

You must be getting excited about your trip to California.

My classes are progressing. We are about to have a test on the relapse section. It's really interesting. All next week, we do something called Beat Street. It takes a week, and then we have a test on Labor Day.

I got your letter today, also pictures of Dennis and Nancy's trip to the Sturgis motorcycle rally. Dennis got his bike painted again.

Urantia sermon was great. Susan placed a Urantia book in the Bellows Falls library in memory of Nebadon.

I signed my progress report today. I got very good recommendations. My prison career has been without blemish so the halfway house won't refuse me. So I got that going for me!

Next week class number 18 will graduate, and we will be seniors. We also get some cake and Kool-Aid.

And the beat goes on. It would be nice to have another visit from you, but I would understand if you can't make it work.

The ban has been lifted on adults-only material. The feds lost the case so we can have postcards again. I just don't know if we can mail them out or not. I'm famous in the mail room. They know me by name. Postcard George, they call me!

That's all for now.

Love,
Me

Charlene,

Today while you were winging your way I was sitting in the visiting room watching class 18 graduate from the DAP drug program. Now I am a senior. Only sixty-three days left to go for me. We are having our relapse module test on Monday. It should only take about half an hour. Then we have a picnic. Next Thursday this class will be on their way to halfway houses. The next class of 28 will be moving over. This class will be the last one that I will see. *Yes*!

I think J. M. will be leaving here on October 17. That's earlier than he thought.

This weekend they are showing *Donnie Brasco*. We sneak previewed it because they sent it early. I saw 90 percent of it, and I loved it. I was watching it with Frankie Garafalo who was pretty high up in the Brooklyn outfit. He said it was very real. I was making fun of the Goombas like I do with Bugs and Owl. Frank has a good sense of humor. I'm still alive, ain't I! "All those Goombas from Brooklyn know is 'Manicotti, manicotti, manicotti'(heh, heh). Fuck you, Wesche," says Frank.

Well, I hope you have fun with your daughter.

Take care.
George

Johnny,

A moment of silence in respect for the passing of a true saint. Mother Terresa will be missed, but her work will be carried on, also Princess Diana. She was a fox. I always liked her. Her funeral is today. I fucked her!

On a lighter note, it's September motherfucker, and time is marching on. Only fifty-four more days in this fucking hole. And I'm ready, ready as anybody can be. I'm ready for you. I hope you are ready for me. I'm drinking TNT. I'm smoking dynamite, I hope some screwball starts a fight. 'Cause I'm ready!

I should know where I am going for halfway house real soon. J. M. is out of here on October 17. I'm out on October 30. We bad! We bad!

I can't think of anything but release. It's had to keep up my routine, but I am still working out.

Pump up...

Love,
Miro

Johnny,

It's official. My new address as of October 30, 1997 is:

> Coolidge House
> 307 Huntington Ave
> Boston Mass 02115

So come on down. I may have a job as a driver.

I drive the big boys to work and the airport. I will be spending the winter at least in Beantown. Forty-four days and a wakeup left.

Clark Terry is the shit! I agree.

I am packing up some stuff right now for the monthly mailing so when I leave here, I will just have the clothes on my back and no money in my pocket.

I got my last treatment plan last week. I am half done. It is very hard to concentrate. It's almost over, and I am like a kid on Christmas eve.

> Peace and love,
> Lou Albano

Kravetz,

Felching a Dead Horse by my favorite group, TV Terror. But I love that dirty water 'cause Boston, your my new home.

Got another letter from Donna. She just came from a Picasso exhibit in Boston. That's one of the first things I would like to do when I am free. Donna says hello to you Bugs and Owl. What a reunion that would be.

I got my halfway house papers and confirmation date. They gave me ten hours to drive six and a half hours. Charlene is picking me up. Oh, baby. Motel hell!

So you saw Brother Brown? Was he all bewildered? Was he on the good foot? Did he sing that little part that might sting you in your heart? Did you scream? Don't say oww, say *oww*! Baby, take my hand. I wanna be your lovin' man!

I think I may have a job buying cars in Vermont and New Hampshire, for a guy out of Springfield Massachusetts.

I got a letter from Lynn today. My mother is sending me some clothes. Only thirty-eight days to go.

I wrote Doc a real long letter, and he never wrote back. I don't know if he got it or not. I will send him my Boston Address.

Well J. M. says hello back to you.

Take care, dude.
Frampton Pinkney

Kravetz,

Why didn't you tell me that you saw Gracie and John at a George Clinton concert? She's so hip mama. It brought a tear to my eye. For all I knew she was a country fan. Grace, you know your *outta site*! Grace is going to look around for some clothes for me. Charlene is going to bring them down when she comes to get me. Since I will be in Boston, I won't be up to Vermont for a while. Travis is back in high school. Grace is at Community College of Vermont and working at Halladay's Florist. And I am in the Big House, but I am almost back baby. Boston will be an adventure, and I am looking forward to it. I'm going to be with some *heavy hitters* and who knows where it will lead.

God, I can't believe Gracie is into P-Funk. I did something right.

Love and kisses,
Bootsy

Letter number 151, FPC Allenwood, October 14, 1997, fifteen days left at Allenwood, to Charlene Wakefield

Hey, baby,

Today I started training my replacement for my orderly job. At the end of this week, I am officially on vacation till I leave. I am tying up loose ends

I am working on finding a job before I get there. I may be a driver, and also I know a guy with a restaurant in the North End. The feds have my driver's license and passport and everything else they confiscated from my safety deposit box. If not it could be up in Chittenden County where they took my Harley. Nebadon took my car before they could get hold of it.

I can't wait for you to get here, and we leave this place. There are no visits on Wednesday night. Too bad. But bright and early Thursday morning, we can leave this place. We can be in Boston in seven hours.

We have one more week in class and then we twiddle our thumbs till graduation. We really do nothing now in class.

I had my fourth AIDS test. They want to make sure that I am not a member of the midnight shower club! I know that the test will be negative. I haven't had sex in three years and five months, but then who's counting.

I am also working on these people to give me some clothes. I may be able to get a jacket.

Still no word from Doc. I will write him again from Boston.

Too bad about Brian. It was depressing. You never hear from him when he is depressed. I don't like to sound too excited around him when he is staying in jail. We never do it here. It's just common courtesy.

Well, honey, I can't wait to see you.

G

Charlene,

I showed some of your artwork to my artist friend, James Langlois. He liked it. He said it was very interesting. Please send me a broken-dish angel postcard so I can give it to him. I would like to have you meet him one day. He is in the class behind me. His wife lives in New Hampshire now, but they are looking to buy a place in Vermont. He is very familiar with the Charlemont, Massachusetts, area. You two may have some mutual acquaintances. Today we got rid of class number eighteen. We are now seniors. Monday class number 22 comes over, and we will be full again.

I just got back from running three miles. Tomorrow is my day off.

On Sunday I hang out with my buddy Jimmy, and we drive the van down to the chapel. Gotta make sure that all the sinners get to church.

Everyone is watching Princess Dianna's funeral today, but the world really experienced a great loss with the passing of Mother Teressa. She truly was a saint. Her work will be carried on. She will be missed.

All I can think about these days is being with you. I have dreams about it.

Love and everything else,
G

Chucky,

I got your police postcard yesterday, and your Haight St. card today. Both were very cool. Everyone liked them. Jim got his halfway house date pushed back. They couldn't find a spot for him in Boston.

Well, I got my halfway house, and it is in Boston. The news is final. I am excited. It's been a long time, since I spent any time in a city. I got the same date October 30 and a bunch of guys from here will be there together.

Boston is a nice place for us to spend some time together.

I got my papers to sign. It's my copy of the rules. It doesn't seem much different than the rules here. They feed us once a day, and I can stay out till 7:00 p.m. with extensions till 9:00 p.m.

I can have overnight and weekend passes as time goes by.

Do you still want to come here and get me? You would be coming here to get me and bringing me to Boston. It would be a great help. I would really appreciate it.

Moe my friend from Springfield, Massachusetts is leaving here on October 3rd, so we would all be there together.

Once I get a job and a savings account, I can get twenty-four-hour and forty-eight-hour passes.

I definitely want to hear about your trip.

Anyway please write and let me know what you think about driving me to Boston.

Love,
G

Yonz,

Que passa?

Lynn says you were on her answering machine when she got home.

Charlene will be here to get me at 8:15 on October 30th. Oh, baby, it's been four years of foreplay! I also got a letter from an old girlfriend letting me know she was single again. What can I say, ladies love outlaws, and I love the ladies.

I can't wait to get to Boston. It is gonna be great. I am looking into jobs from here trying to line something up before I get there.

I'm lifting again, but I don't want to get hurt again. Shoulder is still not 100 percent so I asked one of the *gorillas* down there how much I should do to start. Take it slow was the reply. (Just one to see if you can do it.)

I am reading *Dark Star* right now. It's great. That's all for now. See you later.

Love,
Skylo Low

Dear Charlene,

I am on vacation until I leave but my teacher is having a three-hour class tomorrow. What a pain in the ass. Oh well, we are planning our graduation ceremony. I will be giving a thirty-second talk then we cut the cake. I don't know what flavor.

A good friend of mine left today. Lots of my friends are ready to jump.

So you saw Marilyn. That's good. Next time you see her tell her Brian owes me a letter.

I'm looking forward to our Boston trip. It will be great to spend some time with you. You probably won't be writing me any more letters here seeing as you will be here on Wednesday. It will be good to see you. It's been a long time coming. I can't wait to hold you in my arms.

I got a letter from Bugs tonight. He is back in school studying to be a scientist. He reads a lot.

Sharon and him want to come to visit in Boston.

On Tuesday is graduation and on Wednesday is what they call "walk-around." We have to have all of the departments sign off on us. It takes all day to get the signatures. Then on Thursday morning at 8:30 you come and pick me up. Then off we go to Boston. I just got the results of my fourth AIDS test in four years. I am good to go.

I can't wait to see you.

Love,
G

ABOUT THE AUTHOR

My name is George Wesche.

I am a retired health care worker and member of the counterculture. We moved to Vermont and have been living and working here since the early seventies. Kids are grown and on their own. I am enjoying retirement, but I volunteer some of my time working with the elderly. Life is good.

Lightning Source UK Ltd.
Milton Keynes UK
UKHW010329110223
416808UK00001B/59

9 798886 547634